THE WEDDING VASE

On one of our dates, to a Native American Pow-Wow in Denver, Laurence wanted to buy me a gift. I suggested that we buy something for us, instead of me. He agreed. As we looked around at quilts, dream-catchers, and other possible items we could share as a couple, I spotted a hand-made **wedding vase** made of clay. Laurence hadn't asked me to marry him yet, but the vase still felt right for us. He bought the vase, and we happily brought it home to sit upon the mantel.

I sometimes imagined how we might actually use the vase one day in our wedding ceremony. In Native American tradition, one spout of the vessel represents the husband and the other represents the wife. The looped handle represents the unity of marriage, and the space created within the loop represents the circle of life. In the wedding ceremony, the groom offers the bride the vessel and she sips from one side. The bride then turns the vase clockwise, and the groom sips from the same side. Then they each drink from the opposite side, and then both drink from it together. If the couple can do this, they will have a strong marriage.

Advance Reviews

"Patti Ashley opens the door to the 'back of her heart' giving us an intimate glimpse into her innermost feelings surrounding her life-time journey of love, loss and healing. She expresses the depths of her emotion with fierce courage and raw honesty, inviting us all to bridge the paradox of love and grief within our own lives. BILLIE ORTIZ, WORKSHOP FACILITATOR, DREAM TRAINING MENTOR AND PROFES-SIONAL DREAMWORKER AT *WAKE UP TO YOUR DREAMS*

"A beautiful celebration of snapshots from the life we share with others who are taken from us too soon. A powerful healing journey through story." KRISTEN WHITE, CEO OF WHITE MEDIA PRODUCTIONS, BESTSELLING AUTHOR & AWARD-WINNING MEDIA MARKETING COACH

"Patti has taken the raw material of her grief and transformed it into compassion and understanding, leaving the reader with the grace of hope and belonging." LAURA K. DEAL, PH.D., AUTHOR OF *THE NEW-COMER'S GUIDE TO THE INVISIBLE REALM* AND *A JOURNEY THROUGH DREAMS, METAPHOR AND IMAGINATION*

"Her writing is beautiful, and the style is reminiscent of Jeanette Walls." DR. MARCY COOPER, CHILD PSYCHIATRIST, DENVER, CO

"A love story that makes your heart sing while also feeling the insufferable pain of loss. Her honesty and courageous willingness to share raw, uncensored emotions while grieving has created this remarkable tribute to the human spirit." DONNA V. REMMERT, BOULDER FRIENDS OF JUNG (BFJ) BOARD MEMBER, AND AUTHOR OF *THE LITTLEST BIG KID, THE JITTERBUG GIRL, & HEAD OVER HEELS*

"This memoir is unusually powerful. Even if you didn't know Laurence, his journey will not only inspire you: it has the capacity to impel you, accelerating you on your path of unfoldment." DR. ROGER TEEL, AUTHOR OF *THIS LIFE IS JOY*

"This lovely book is a must-read for anyone grappling with the death of a loved one." DR. M. WILLSON WILLIAMS, DEAN (RET.), COLLEGE OF SOCIAL SCIENCES, SAYBROOK UNIVERSITY; PROFESSOR EMERITA, UNION INSTITUTE & UNIVERSITY

"Patti shares her raw journey through love and grief in a way that only a true spiritual seeker can do. Her blend of psychology and spirituality makes this book a resource for anyone finding their way through loss and heartbreak." SUE FREDERICK, AUTHOR OF *BRIDGES TO HEAVEN: TRUE STORIES OF LOVED ONES ON THE OTHER SIDE*

"Patti Ashley offers tender, comforting and compassionate understanding of the deep life-changing grief that sometimes follows a deep life-changing loving relationship. And most important of all, she gives us reason to continue loving with our whole heart." SANDRA FELT, LCSW, PSYCHOTHERAPIST AND AUTHOR OF *BEYOND THE GOOD-GIRL JAIL*

"A poignant and beautifully soulful love story." DR. ANNAMARIE FIDEL-RICE, AUTHOR OF *THE ALCHEMY OF GRIEF: EMBRACING MOURNING THROUGH GRACE*

"Patti has brought to us the spark of divinity that lights this whole Universe in this sharing of her heart's journey. It is a journey worth the time to dream into. As Laurence wrote in his poem—*your true mission is to remember the love that you are and to extend this love to all those around you*—this book is love's 'extension." LEE R. MCCORMICK, AUTHOR OF *THE SPIRIT RECOVERY MEDITATION JOURNAL*

"A masterful story of heart and grace, as a result of her time gathering meaning and greater understanding of the losses upon her life path. Life is a love story opening our hearts to freedom." PATTY LUCKENBACH, DD, AUTHOR OF *THE LAND OF TEARS IS A SECRET PLACE, THE KINGDOM OF HEART,* AND *I ONLY WALK ON WATER WHEN IT RAINS*

Letters *to* Freedom

FROM
FEAR
TO
LOVE
TO
GRACE

Letters *to* Freedom

FROM
FEAR
TO
LOVE
TO
GRACE

PATTI ASHLEY, PH.D., LPC

Wyatt-MacKenzie Publishing
DEADWOOD, OREGON

Letters to Freedom
From Fear to Love to Grace
Patti Ashley, Ph.D., LPC

Softcover Edition ISBN: 978-1-948018-45-6
Library of Congress Control Number: 2019932303

Wyatt-MacKenzie Publishing
DEADWOOD, OREGON

For Laurence

Table of Contents

PART THREE

Grace

APPENDIX

Foreword

You are reading a book about a rare and wonderful being: Laurence Freedom. I loved Laurence but, even more, I hold his memory and essence in great respect. As with us all, his life was so much more than a compilation of dates and data. His life was a soul-guided journey, one that became a great blessing to many others.

I invite you to read this life story with an open heart, sensing into the rich, deep, and often agonizing elements of the hero's journey. Laurence engaged in the single moments of his unique journey with deliberate willingness and the intention to use it all for personal transformation and soulful emergence. And true heroes always direct and actualize their growth in service to others. Laurence accomplished this so naturally and generously as a preeminent addiction counselor, devoted sponsor, and spiritual guide. So many lives felt this healing touch at his recovery centers.

What is so impressive about Laurence's journey was his unquenchable thirst for understanding and spiritual development. No doubt this was grist from the mill gleaned from his phases of struggle. He eventually arrived at a willingness to stretch the envelope of his awareness and to surrender himself at the edge of his greater yet-to-be. All along the way, Laurence also shared his humor, compassion, honesty, and joy. It was a pleasure and privilege to be around him!

This memoir is unusually powerful. Even if you didn't know Laurence, his journey will not only inspire you: it has the capacity to impel you, accelerating you on your path of unfoldment. How perfect that Laurence's surname was *Freedom!* His life story is a request for us all to claim our inner freedom and to unleash what Robert Browning called our "imprisoned splendor." Let's accept his invitation. I am certain that the Light Being we knew here as Laurence Freedom will let loose a great celebration!

DR. ROGER TEEL
Spiritual Leader and Author of *This Life is Joy: Discovering the Spiritual Laws to Live More Powerfully, Lovingly, and Happily*

Preface

*"I do not at all understand the mystery of grace. Only, that it meets us where
we are but does not leave us where it found us."*

ANNE LAMOTT

For the first few months after my beloved Laurence Freedom died, all I could do was write down our stories. They seemed to belong somewhere. So many synchronicities and events I wanted to remember.

Those stories have since become this book.

One thing I learned about grief in my counselor training was that we have to tell the story at least one hundred times before we can begin to move on to acceptance (of sorts). After Laurence died, I didn't want to burden my friends with my endless lamenting. So instead, I sat down night after night for many months; remembering, writing, and dripping tears onto my computer's keyboard.

I thought I knew grief. What did I know, really?

I knew that losing my beloved hurt, *like hell.*

I am sharing this very vulnerable and intimate story in the hopes that it will help at least one person along the arduous path of grief. Grief is a hard taskmaster: one that I believe truly deepens us, and can bring us back to life, if fully embraced.

The similarities of how Laurence and my father died seem to not be merely a coincidence, but rather very poignant and important parts of my life's learning. Ones, that I hope will continue to inform my work as a therapist.

This is also a book about relationship and dependency. I bravely share my journey of moving from fear to love, and love to grace, as I tell a few stories of how codependency has shown up in my life and has been a major part of my healing. Codependency was also a significant part of what Laurence and I were healing together.

Laurence was writing a book about codependency and relationship prior to his death. I am fortunate to have edited pieces of his writing and still have them on my computer. In his honor, I lovingly share some of them with you in this memoir.

I've learned in my professional and personal life that many people naturally prefer to avoid conversations about emotional pain. Maybe they numb out with addictive behaviors, try to talk themselves out of it, etc. The truth is: we have to go through grief and pain to get to the other side. We can't go around it. It ultimately can bring us collateral joy and beauty, if only we are willing to face the depths of its darkness.

Laurence was loved deeply by many people. He wanted to help everyone see the light of who they truly are. I believe he helped me write this book for you. So in a way, he is my co-author. I know he is forever guiding me on this *magical mystery ride.* Here is a quote from his writing that sums up how Laurence saw our journey here on planet earth:

> *You were an expression of love before you were born.*
> *You will return into love when you pass.*
> *Between your first and last breath,*
> *your true mission is to remember the love that you are*
> *and to extend this love to all those around you.*
> LAURENCE FREEDOM

THE LAST LETTER

Letter #7
November 13, 2016
(Watching the Broncos without you)

Dearest Laurence:

Last night I remembered the moment I asked my father not to go to work. The unspoken tension in the house that day was extra heavy. I was only eleven. *"Please don't go to work tomorrow,"* I whispered.

The next day, my sister found him gasping for his last breath on the living room floor. He had been scraping the ice and snow off his car trying to get to work that day.

I can still see Daddy and me, face to face, in the same spot of the house where once he got out his belt to spank me. He never hit me. Instead, he put the belt away.

He was a gentle soul and could do no harm. I was lucky to have a father like that. Especially compared to some of my friends' dads, who were often angry and sometimes abusive. Not my dad.

I am so worried you might not want to be in a relation-ship with me anymore. I wonder why I am so anxious. Is it the little girl who asked Daddy not to go to work and he did anyway? And then he died.

I had a father who loved me more than life itself, and in an instant, he was gone. You promised to never leave me, and yet today I am so afraid you are gone.

I love you more than words can say. I am counting the days until I see you again.

Always,
Your Ladybug

I finished this last letter to Laurence on the morning of November 13, 2016, right before receiving the call from Jim.

"Laurence is dead. I found him on the floor of his house. He missed an appointment yesterday and didn't answer his phone. I went over to check on him and found him dead on the floor."

"What? No. What? No. Who found him? No. What? NO. That can't be true. We had a date next week to talk about how we were going to move forward in our relationship. I was writing him love letters and putting them in a special hand-painted box. What? No. What? No, no, no! That can't be true."

PART ONE

Fear

*"I warn you: this will not be easy. I warn you: this will take some work.
I warn you: love will burn you up. Are you ready to be burned,
or would you rather just grow old?"*

MARIANNE WILLIAMSON, *Enchanted Love*

A Mistake

My mother adored my father. Over and over, she would tell the story about the day he returned from World War II and asked her to marry him, like a precious scene from the best chapter of her life.

My parents met in high school. My mom sometimes called my dad a *soda jerk*. It was a common label in their teen years. A *soda jerk* was similar to a bartender, serving up fancy sundaes, floats, and sodas. The jerking action of the arm while making sodas inspired the name.

My mom stayed single into her early thirties, even though she had many suitors. None compared to my father. Not a day went by that she didn't think of him. Women in the 1940s were considered spinsters if they hadn't married by the time they turned thirty. That didn't matter to my mother because her heart belonged to Clem. My dad.

My maternal grandfather owned and operated the first movie theatre in my hometown of Norfolk, Virginia. My mother sold tickets at the box office. One seemingly typical day, she looked up and saw Clem there.

"The army doesn't want me anymore. Do you?" He said, grinning from ear to ear.

They married within months. Nine months later my brother was born. Three years after that my sister was born. Then I came along eight years later. Clearly a mistake.

One night when I was seven or eight years old, my mother introduced me to some of her friends who were playing cards in our living room as *our mistake*. Heading off to bed, I wondered what had happened that made me the mistake. What did I do so wrong?

I don't remember much of my childhood, but I do remember being with my dad. That's where I belonged. With him I never felt like a mistake. I felt like a queen.

Sundays

Sunday mornings, Daddy would wake up before Mom, to make coffee and pancakes. He would always let me help him make the pancakes. He taught me how to wait for the right amount of bubbles to emerge before turning them over.

The coffee he could never quite conquer. We had a stovetop peculator-type coffee pot that would always boil over. Coffee would run down the sides of the pot onto the stove-top. When my mom arrived, she would try to fake that she was happy he had made coffee. But I always knew she was a bit upset. He made a very messy mistake. Nonetheless, I knew she never thought that *he* was a mistake.

After breakfast Daddy and I would sit together in his big brown leather recliner and he would read me the colorful Sunday comics. My favorite was *Peanuts*.

Most Sundays we would go to visit Aunt Lula in Portsmouth after church. What I mostly remember of those Sunday drives was the very strong smell of bread baking at the Mary Jane Bakery, followed by a ride through the Portsmouth tunnel. First the pleasant fragrance, and then the dark mystery of the underwater tunnel, consistently and rhythmically every trip.

In September 2017, the local newspaper *The Virginian-Pilot* featured an article about the smell of the closing bakery:

The shifting winds would carry the smell for miles, covering Norfolk neighborhoods with a scent that would seal itself into our memories. The unmistakable smell of freshly baked bread. The Mary Jane Bakery appeared in Norfolk in early 1937. The bread can still be found on the shelves of some stores in the area, but the smell and the memories of this local bread are gone forever (Hays & Watts).

My father had been raised by Lula. I'm not fully aware of why. What I do know is that his mother owned a nightclub in North Carolina with her second husband. She previously had been a singer in New York. My father never knew his father. Even though my sister-in-law recently discovered in her genealogy research that he had lived very close by. Sad for me to think about that. I wonder what it must have been like for him to not have much of a relationship with his mother or father. He was quite a family man and loved us all very much.

The Sunday visits with Lula and her son Howard consisted first of sitting properly in the living room and having grown-up types of conversations. Then we would move to the formal dining room, where I distinctly remember the delicately painted fragile dishes. I was especially curious about the tiny salt and pepper shakers. I anxiously studied the proper etiquette needed to perform the precise orchestration of passing the salt. After all, I was the mistake, so I better not make one!

My preferred Sundays were the ones when we didn't have to go to Portsmouth. Instead, my dad took me to City Park. Just the two of us. I especially liked it when he would let me run through the water that came up out of the ground from small holes. It would shoot straight up a few feet into the air, and then cascade back down, creating an exciting water park-like adventure.

On Sunday afternoons we would all take a nap. When we got up, Mom made us sandwiches because we had had our *big meal* mid-day; usually fried chicken and mashed potatoes. Sundays would end happily with me back in my dad's lap, watching Ed Sullivan and Jackie Gleason on our black and white TV.

My father not only was kind, he was also very funny. He had a dry sense of humor that made me smile and sigh at the same time. He was known for his expressions, such as: *Put that in your pipe and smoke it; You're full of bologna;* and *Not until Patti goes into the army.* They were usually said in the context of following up on some information he had shared, or in response to a question or comment. As a child, I really had no idea what they meant, but his endearing comments would always make me smile.

Rascal

Every night around five o'clock I would hide in the hall closet waiting for my father to come home from work. The first thing he did when he arrived was put his coat and his money box away in that closet. I would sit on the clothes hamper anxiously anticipating his arrival. Listening for the back door to open and the sound of his footsteps down the hall, I perched like a cat on the edge of my seat.

When he opened the closet door, I'd jump up and shout, *"BOO!"*

He always acted scared. We laughed and hugged hello. That was our evening ritual.

One night while sitting in the closet waiting for my dad, I heard the phone ring, the rotary dial one that was attached to the wall in the kitchen. It had an extra-long cord so that my mother could talk and cook at the same time. I still remember our number: 623-2495.

"Does it have long hair? Is it well-behaved? Who's going to take care of it? (silence) Oh, okay, all right."

A few months prior I had asked Santa for a puppy, but I didn't get one. My father loved to spoil me at Christmas. I'm sure he was hoping to make up for Santa's failure, and at the same time, help out his friend. My father loved to help people. His friend needed to find a home for a medium-sized terrier-mutt dog that looked a bit like Benjie. The friend had told my dad that his wife said it was either her or the dog.

I stayed in the closet for a while longer that night. I never let him know that I'd overheard the conversation he had with my mom on the phone. I was so happy to finally have my dog *Rascal*.

And he was definitely a rascal! I guess the reason the man had to get rid of him was that he chewed everything up! He growled, barked, and a few times bit people on walks. I spent a lot of time training him. After a few years, he was the best dog anyone could imagine. He became my best buddy. He greeted me every day when I returned home and never left my side. One of the many sweet things I remember about Rascal is how he would sit up on his hind legs at the dinner table and patiently wait for a treat. He was a very special pal.

I am not sure if my mom ever learned to truly love Rascal. However, as she typically loved everything and everyone, I imagine she came to love him, too. Dogs, to me, represent unconditional love. My mom certainly was a woman who loved that way. As the saying goes... *She never met a stranger!*

Sadly, one day, I remember staying home from school, sleeping on the sofa bed in the living room because I was too sick to go upstairs. That day felt eerily quiet and lonely. Later in the afternoon, my mom casually told me that Rascal was sick. They had taken him to the doctor. He was not coming home. That was the end of the conversation.

I don't know why no one told me he had been sick, and that they were going to euthanize him. I guess they wanted to spare me the pain by not talking about it. But again, I was *the mistake*. I wasn't going to question anything or anyone.

The Chesapeake Bay

My parents had friends who owned a home on the Chesapeake Bay. We spent many weekends there on the beach. My sister and I would sleep on rollaway beds on the screened-in porch. The sound of the waves crashing on the shore was such a soothing experience. The lights of the Chesapeake Bay Bridge Tunnel off in the distance twinkled like stars. I very much enjoyed spending time there.

My sister and I took big crab-pots out at low tide and then picked them up during the next day's low tide, with them full of the crustaceans. The adults boiled them, and we all sat around the kitchen table for hours, cracking crabs: some to eat and some to put in the freezer. I never tired of crab. Still to this day it is one of my favorite foods.

I sometimes played with my friends on the beach. We made ice cream cones out of sand and paper cups. My dad paid us a nickel for each one. It was always fun.

I swam in the bay as often as I could, but one scary day I almost drowned. The underwater sand was being dredged up and put onto the beach to replace the eroding shoreline. I fell into a hole and couldn't swim out. I grabbed my friend and together she doggy-paddled us to shallow water.

We were yelling for help, but my mom thought we were joking. When we got to the sandy shore, we were very shaken, and glad to be alive. The incident didn't keep me from swimming, though. Mom signed me up for swim lessons, and I was confident after that.

Double Figures

I remember turning ten. *Double figures*, my dad said. I wasn't a big sports fan at the time, so I wasn't exactly sure why that was important. What it meant to me was that I was growing up. Adding another digit to my age. I was older, but I still felt like a mistake.

I don't remember much about that year except that the Sunday trips to Portsmouth and the park were less common than before. My dad had a bed set up in the dining room because the doctors said he had hardening of the arteries and could no longer walk up the stairs.

That was all I knew.

I wasn't told much about my father's heart disease. I suppose it was my family's way of protecting me from the painful truth: *my father was dying.*

What I heard in the silence was the fear that he was getting worse. His heart was having difficulty carrying his excess weight. Still, he refused to stop the midnight snacks and the morning bacon and egg breakfasts at the local diner on the way to work. One night I remember looking up at him and saying, "Please don't go to work tomorrow." He smiled, nodded, and walked away.

The next morning, I woke up to hear the newsperson announce that the local university was closed due to the snow. In our coastal town, snow was a rare event. The public schools closed for as little as an inch or two. The colleges, however usually stayed open. I knew it had to be a pretty big snow if Old Dominion University (ODU) was closed.

"Sissy, you don't have school today," I yelled in a loud voice from my upstairs room. The somber response from my mother was, "Patti, put on your robe and come downstairs."

My excitement about a snow day soon turned to trepidation about what my mom wanted from me. Did I make a *mistake*? What could have possibly happened to make such a good snow day go so bad?

I put on my robe and slippers and walked down the winding staircase. My mother was standing at the bottom of the steps with a police officer beside her. I looked to my left and saw a large lump the size of my father, covered in a green blanket on the living room floor.

The only thing I remember after that was my sister trying to get the priest from the church across the street, in the snowstorm, through icy, torn-up roads under construction. Then sitting at the kitchen table with a piece of toast in front of me, which my mother told me I had to eat. The last thing I wanted to do was to eat toast.

The next day, my brother flew in from Arizona with his wife and one-year old daughter. My friends stopped by. I was grateful the baby was there to shift the focus away from something too big for me to process.

At the funeral, I didn't cry. I thought there must be something wrong with me. Why couldn't I cry? I learned much later in graduate school that I was in shock. What a relief to know I wasn't a freak. Shock is a normal reaction to sudden death: too much to take in. The body has to shut down, like it does in a severe accident with bodily injuries. We don't feel any pain because it is too intense. We feel it later. Little by little over a long period of time.

My father was fifty-eight when he died. I was eleven. I would be turning twelve in July. For a long while I said I was twelve, while I was still only eleven. I wanted to be grown up and able to handle my father's dying like a *big girl*.

Double figures... I was definitely older than the year before.

Sixth Grade

One week after my father died, I went back to my sixth-grade classroom. I attended the parochial school across the street from our house. My father bought the house for my mother when they found out about *the mistake.* With three children, he wanted to make it easier for her, by living within walking distance to church and school. We lived so close that I could hear the school bell ring from my backyard.

The Catholic faith was strong on my mother's side of the family. My grandmother had also been widowed young. They both had several statues of the Blessed Mother on altars in their bedrooms, surrounded by roses, medals, and prayer cards. My father had converted to Catholicism for my mother, and he went to church with us every Sunday. But, some Sundays he would volunteer as an usher at the early morning service, so he could spend more time with us later in the day.

When my father died, I was told he was in Heaven, and that he was fortunate to be with Jesus, Mary, and all the Saints. *Be happy for him,* they said. He had attained *eternal life.*

Happy was *not* what I was feeling. Was that a mistake?

Only a few things from sixth grade stand out in my memory. I don't remember much. I must have been out of my body most of the time, wishing I was in Heaven with my dad. The Catholic Church taught us that if you commit suicide, you go to hell. That wasn't an option, although I thought about it now and again. Life without my dad would never, ever be the same.

One thing I remember about school after he died was a reading exercise being projected onto the board. The class had to read each sentence out-loud together. I was having a difficult time following along. Sister Christina came around with her pink notepad and wrote that I wasn't paying attention in class. I was punished. Maybe it was a wake-up call, to the fact that I needed to come back down to earth and be in my body. I had to accept that no one was going to help me process my grief. I didn't even know that was what I needed. I was the mistake.

Another memory is one day in religion class, I had joined my friends in projecting spitballs at Fr. Drake. He wore strappy sandals with socks and was a bit awkward. Several of my friends were making fun of him. Even though I joined in, Sister Christina felt sorry for me because my father had just died. I was the only one who didn't get suspended. My friends were jealous.

In fifth grade I had started practicing for cheerleading tryouts. Sixth grade was the year I could finally join the squad. I practiced every day. I clapped and screamed and jumped and hollered often, both in and outside of the house. My dad often called me *Cheers.*

I continued to cheer all through high school, making captain my senior year. Since my father died when I was in sixth grade, he never got to see me cheer at a basketball game.

When I look back on those days, I imagine that being involved in that type of physical and vocal expression helped me release some of the feelings I was carrying in my body surrounding the grief.

Mixed messages. Confusion. Uncertainty. A black hole entryway into adolescence.

Stop Crying Before I Give You Something to Cry About

"Stop crying before I give you something to cry about," was a common remark made in my family. My mother was never comfortable with tears or complaints. I typically felt it wasn't okay to cry or be sad.

Even though I had been taught not to cry, almost everyone was crying at my father's funeral. Somehow, I couldn't cry. I thought there must be something wrong with me. Why couldn't I shed a tear?

I felt ashamed.

I also felt confused because my mother was now crying *a lot*.

The week after my father died, I can recall standing in the upstairs hallway, outside of my mother's bedroom. She didn't know I was there. She was crying. Wailing, actually. The woman who had taught me to stop crying couldn't stop herself this time. It sounded like she was hyperventilating. This went on for hours. I stood there listening. She never knew.

I vividly remember declaring to myself in that moment, *I will never love anyone that much, because I never want to feel that much pain.*

A few months later, I bought my mom a plaque with the Serenity Prayer embroidered on it. She hung it over her bed. I'm not sure if I was now becoming *her* caretaker, or if I was just taking care of myself. Maybe it was a little of both.

> *"God grant me the serenity to accept the things I can't change.*
> *The courage to change the things I can,*
> *and the wisdom to know the difference."*
> REINHOLD NIEBUR

A Fatherless Teen

In seventh grade, Sister Claire came to teach math at our school. She was so cool. She talked to us like we were real people, unlike most of the other nuns who were shaming and punitive. Claire was kind. She truly cared about her students.

Every day after lunch we went to the playground and swarmed around her like bees. We couldn't get close enough to her. She was the best. She brought contemporary music and dance into the church. She choreographed modern dance performances and danced down the aisles during Sunday services. She was radical.

I remember some of the gifts she gave us on various occasions. The book *Jonathan Livingston Seagull* by Richard Bach, a story about a seagull who strives to fly high above the normal life of his peers; a silver cross pendent that I wore almost every day for years; and a card that said: "We find ourselves in the quiet moments, when the earth pauses, and we are still." She wanted us all to thrive, not merely survive.

Sr. Claire offered after-school guitar lessons and created a folk group that sang at the eleven o'clock mass on Sunday. I signed up for both. We learned songs from *Godspell,* and *Jesus Christ Superstar*, as well as music written by social activists such as David Crosby, John Prine, and Joni Mitchell.

The folk group consisted of seventh graders and up. My mother, of course, assumed that the church group was a safe place for me to spend many of my evenings and weekends. But she didn't know what was happening behind the church after choir practice: two older boys flirting with me and my friend, Pam. Eventually, the flirting turned into something my father would not have liked me doing at the early age of thirteen.

When Sister Claire found out, she gathered us together and slammed the classroom door yelling, "This needs to stop!" She told us the behavior she was hearing about was not okay.

I didn't listen.

Sex, drugs, and rock-in-roll became my secret life.

Cheerleading and the church group was my life that everyone else saw.

My mother never questioned why I was coming home late from folk group practice. Maybe in her grief, she hadn't noticed.

By the time I got to high school, in what appeared to be my *real* life, I was a head cheerleader; a good Catholic girl; and a medical assistant to a local physician after school. Little did anyone know that marijuana, cheap wine, and older boys had become the secret I was driven to hide. In my mind, I was all grown up.

High school was difficult for me. By the end of my senior year I was falling asleep in the school library and struggling to graduate. Luckily, I had taken myself to Planned Parenthood on my sixteenth birthday to get birth control. Had I not, this might be a completely different story.

Sad was my new normal. I didn't know any different. I couldn't understand the humor in the slapstick comedies my peers were watching. How could they laugh about people farting around a campfire in the popular movie. *Blazing Saddles*? To me, life was not funny. It was seriously hard.

I remember one day on the bus going to work after school, a man said to me, "Smile. You look so sad." I didn't even know there was another way to be. I missed my dad terribly. But I never talked about it.

It was then that I first thought about becoming a therapist. I wanted to give people a place to talk about things that no one else wanted to talk about. When I told the guidance counselor that I wanted to be a psychologist, she told me I would need a Ph.D. and I wasn't smart enough for that.

So much for giving people a place to talk about things they don't want to talk about.

I barely graduated. I had no future plans. At the last minute, I applied to Virginia Commonwealth University (VCU) a nearby college, because my mother told me I would continue to get my father's social security benefits if I was still in school.

I arrived that fall, sleeping in a room reserved for students without dorm rooms, similar to flying stand-by on a plane. The college expected a number of students to withdraw within the first few weeks of school, and then the rooms would be available for those of us sleeping in the temporary bunk room.

Sophomore year, I transferred to James Madison University (JMU) located in the mountains of Virginia, and I enrolled in a four-year special education major, which would allow me to teach children with emotional problems. I thought that it was close enough to a psychologist, and it took much less schooling, and JMU had a good education department.

Finally, I had a little more direction. However, I always was a bit lost and unsure of why I had to be on the planet, when my father was not.

In 2014, I pondered the question of what my life might have been like if my father had been around during my teen years. Here's a portion of a blog I wrote about that question:

The Day After Father's Day

How would my life have been different if I had had a father beyond the age of eleven? What would it have been like to bring home my first date? What would Dad have said? How would he have protected me, held my hand, and told the boys not to hurt his little girl?

Maybe every child needs a dad like that. Someone who is always there for her and never gives up on her. Someone who is strong and takes care of her and watches her grow into a woman, and then launches her out into the world.

I was lucky to have that dad for eleven years. Some girls don't get along with their fathers. They grow up and become estranged from them for different reasons. Abuse, neglect, misunderstandings, and dysfunctional family patterns can make father-daughter relationships challenging.

Instead I have a fantasy of what my father might have been like, based on my first eleven years. Most of all, I remember Sundays.

Sunday was always the best day of the week. He was always there. We would start the day with the Sunday comics... oh, but first we would make pancakes and coffee...

Some very special and rare weekdays he would take me to work with him, inspecting houses for new insulation. I remember one winter when he taught me that if the snow stayed on a roof and took a while to melt, then that was a house with good insulation. I still look at rooftops in the snow and think of my dad's knowledge. I thought he was very smart.

My father taught me to seek my life's purpose, to always strive for the best, and to love with all my heart and then love some more. What greater gift is there in this life? He also taught me that we have hard things in life that we have to get through, and that we all need a safe place to fall.

Four Kids and Fourteen Years Later

During my senior year at JMU, I reconnected with one of the older guys from my church group. I got pregnant and we married a few months later. I had doubts about marrying him and cried on my wedding day. Nonetheless I felt I had to go through with it because it was the right thing to do since I was pregnant.

My marriage was challenged from the start. Carrying fear, guilt, and regret from my earlier *party* days, I went to confession and asked the priest to forgive all my sins. Then I made a vow I was committed not to break. *'Till death do us part.* I wanted to be the good Catholic girl I was *supposed* to be!

Being a mother became my life, and I was devoted to being a *perfect* mother. I continued to make babies, because I loved the experience of birth, and the early childhood *cuteness.*

Many years into my marriage someone reminded me that one day my kids were going to grow up and leave home. It would then just be me and my husband. That was a stark awakening. I wanted a best friend as my life partner to grow old with, and I knew that my husband could never be that. The marriage never felt quite right. At times, he was abusive, and I learned to keep my mouth shut to avoid waking the tiger. I kept hoping maybe it would get better, or maybe it wasn't as bad as it seemed.

Turning thirty, I had to face the reality that he was not my best life partner.

I started graduate school and therapy.

Since I had given up drugs and alcohol when I got pregnant, I assumed I was clean and sober. However, in therapy, I discovered a new addiction: *codependency.*

I remember a poem I wrote at that time, which began: *When I love you more than me, I lose.* In therapy, I began to see my patterns of taking care of everyone else, and not paying attention to my own needs.

I learned that codependency is a form of addiction. When someone pays more attention to the needs of others it can numb out pain, similar to using drugs and alcohol. The difference is that codependency appears to be a *good* thing. Helping people is important, right? Yet, when we over-give, it is actually destructive and addictive behavior. Tough to recognize.

In therapy I learned how to pay attention to what I needed, and how to set healthy boundaries.

Years later, I filed for divorce.

It was brutal.

Guilt became my new life partner for a long time.

Nonetheless, I knew I needed to create a more authentic life for myself and my four children. A long road of heartache and struggle followed.

Looking for Love in All the Wrong Places

Four years after my divorce, I made another huge life decision. I moved to Colorado.

I had dreamed of living in the Rocky Mountains ever since middle school. I vividly recall singing Dan Fogelberg songs on my front porch with a dear friend who lived two blocks down from my childhood home. We had been taking guitar lessons with Sister Claire at the time, but I couldn't quite master the art. I was happy to have my friend bring over his guitar to practice the songs he was learning; he was much more talented than I. As I sang along with him, I could somehow feel the crisp, clear, dry air, and see the bright, blue sky and sharp mountain peaks. Visions and dreams of Colorado stayed with me all those years.

After four years of being divorced, I wondered. *What if?*

I had lost my job at Pediatric Specialists when they were bought-out by the local children's hospital and had recently started working on my doctorate in psychology. With Colorado still on my mind, I discovered it was easier to become a therapist and get my counseling license in Colorado than in the conservative Commonwealth of Virginia.

Colorado offered a new life in a beautiful place.

I hoped that my children and I could live *happily-ever-after* the divorce, two thousand miles away. However, that was a somewhat misguided fantasy, as the move resulted in several years of nasty custody battles. Over time my two youngest children came to live with me, but not without a fight.

I met Ken a few days after I arrived in Colorado. I was listening to live music at the Evergreen Hotel in Morrison, and I saw him from across the room. We went outside to talk. He seemed like a kind and gentle soul, and I wanted to get to know him better. He was ten years younger than I, but neither of us seemed to mind. He had no children, but surprisingly seemed okay knowing that I had four.

One of our first dates was a Super Bowl party at his friend's house.

That was the second year the Denver Broncos won the Super Bowl with John Elway as quarterback. I knew nothing about football and had no previous desire to learn. The Broncos won. I drove home that night watching huge firework displays in the sky, as if it was New Year's Eve or the Fourth of July. The next day, I watched the parade of players and cheerleaders in downtown Denver, close to the office where I worked at the time. It was a big blue and orange festival. I had never lived in a major league town; I became a big Broncos fan, and I have been ever since.

My relationship with Ken was on and off for seven years.

I loved being with him. He called himself an *"enginerd."* We didn't have a whole lot in common except music and our love of Colorado, but I liked his gentle ways. He was quiet and kind. Like my father. And he was funny. Like my dad. We loved to banter back and forth, sharing our dry senses of humor.

Like me, he also had been raised Catholic and had one brother and one sister. We were both labeled *the baby* in our families. His sister lived close to my mother in Virginia and attended her church. That was a strange coincidence. He and his family were from Illinois. His sister had moved to Virginia for a job at American Airlines a few years before Ken and I met.

We enjoyed learning about each other. He was curious and a bit intimidated by my work as a therapist. I was in awe of his ability to design heating and cooling systems. Way too much math for my brain. He was logic and reason. I was heart.

Together we grew in many ways. It was easy being with Ken. I loved him a lot.

We bought a house together. My two youngest children finally came to live with us after long and harsh custody battles, resulting from the Colorado move a few years prior. All my dreams had now come true: my love, my children, and our beautiful house. I had it all.

Nine months later he came home and told me that he was moving back to his other house because things weren't working for him. Even though we had had some disagreements, I thought we were doing the best any couple could do adjusting to living together. I didn't see it coming. He literally swore on a Bible that he wasn't seeing anyone else. The Bible fell out of his hands and onto the floor of my home office. I left it there for weeks, stepping around it, all the while thinking he was lying, and that is why he *dropped* it.

I begged him to stay, but he left anyway.

My daughter had recently left for college. After Ken left, my youngest son and I moved down the road to a rental home. I grieved for many years, as this one hurt really bad.

The following year, Ken e-mailed to tell me he was moving in with a woman he'd been in love with for ten years. I asked, "The lesbian in Florida?" Sure enough, I was right.

He had told me about this friend when we first met. I always knew he had a crush on her, but when she left her husband and moved to Florida with a woman, I no longer thought she was a threat.

She came to Colorado the Christmas after Ken and I bought our house. They went skiing together. I wasn't concerned, because I assumed they were just *friends.* I was wrong and naïve.

 Now he was hers. Not mine.

The same day I got Ken's e-mail, my youngest son boarded a plane to Virginia to live again with his father after graduating from high school that year.

So much for my *happier-ever-after* dream.

Big grief again. I wasn't sure how I would make it. Alone in Colorado with Dan Fogelberg playing on the stereo. That's all I had. No children. No partner. No beautiful house.

I was sad to hear the news when Fogelberg died a few years later of prostate cancer. He had moved to New England years before; now another part of my life had ended. Nonetheless, his music lives on in my heart. One lesson that I learned from grief is that the music never dies.

Two years later I started seeing another younger man that I met at a Susan Tedeschi concert in Boulder. He wanted children of his own. I wasn't going to be the one to do that for him, so our relationship was destined to fail. I stayed in it for two years, trying to convince myself I didn't need anyone to stay. They never had before.

When he moved back east to be closer to his family, I made a decision. I was going to stop looking for love in all the wrong places. I was going to spend some time alone. I was going to see what I really wanted and explore what was keeping me from having a healthy, sustainable relationship.

Then along came Freedom.

PART TWO
Love

"At the heart of love lies an irreducible mystery.
To demystify love is to lose it. Its mystery provides its vital power
to enchant us, to touch us, and to heal us."

MARIANNE WILLIAMSON, *Enchanted Love*

The First Handshake

A few months after moving to Colorado, I was introduced to *Laurence Freedom*. I was finishing up my graduate degree while working at a local psychiatric hospital doing intake evaluations. My friend Amber worked in the marketing department of the hospital and frequently brought in people who worked in the community for us to meet as possible referral sources for our patients.

I remember meeting Laurence more vividly than anyone else who came into my office. I'm not sure why.

He had big blue eyes. I remember shaking his firm hand, while looking into his eyes, saying: "Laurence Freedom."

I thought he had an interestingly powerful name, and he seemed like a very kind man.

I was in my off-and-on romance with Ken at the time and wasn't at all interested in dating other people. Even though the first hello with Laurence was striking, I never thought of him as a potential boyfriend. I didn't know his relationship status at the time, but soon discovered he had recently gotten married to Suzan.

After finishing my doctoral degree, I joined a group practice where Laurence had an office. For several years we shared that space. I can still see his business cards on the file cabinet next to the sofa: *Laurence Freedom, M.Ed., LAC, LPC.*

I also ran into him often at Mile Hi Church, the spiritual home where I would go for support through life's losses and changes.

Our lives seemed to frequently intersect.

Several years later he and Suzan, opened *The Freedom Center*, an out-patient treatment center for addiction in Lakewood, Colorado. I respected Laurence's work and often referred to him as the best in the field. He was an excellent networker. He held meetings once a month, bringing in speakers and giving people opportunities to share their gifts and talents with one another.

He supported my practice by distributing flyers for my workshops, and business cards for my counseling services. He understood my struggles of trying to build a private practice and being self-employed.

I never once thought of him as a romantic partner. He was so in love with Suzan and very committed to her.

Seventeen years after Laurence and I first met, I received a group e-mail from him relaying that his beloved Suzan was in the hospital. She had been diagnosed with a brain tumor. One month after an unsuccessful surgery, she passed away.

I sat alone and cried all through the memorial service at Mile Hi Church. I had never before witnessed the type of committed partnership and devotion that Laurence and Suzan had found. I imagined it was devastating to lose someone so suddenly like that.

After the service, I had to wait in line for almost an hour to give him my condolences. People were lined up outside the community center door and all the way down the hallway. Suzan and he both served as practitioners of the church. They were loved by many people.

Put Yourself Out There

By my fiftieth birthday, I had lost my forties, my mother, my psychotherapy office, and my boyfriend of two years.

It was a year of big losses and more pain.

It was also a year of beginnings.

I had embraced the pain of being alone, the longing to have that special someone, and my past obsessions of trying to find him. Instead of looking for the next *wrong* man, I learned to be still. I became acutely aware of what it meant to love myself, an elusive idea that I hadn't learned in my sacrificial, and somewhat codependent, Catholic background.

I spent the next five years in a relationship with me.

I taught myself how to paint; I danced in my friend Kendra's *Planet Motion* funky dance class several times a week; I listened to live music outside under the beautiful Colorado sky. I met my friend Billie Ortiz, who introduced me to her group of dream-workers.

I bought my first house in June of 2012. To celebrate my fifty-fifth birthday and my new home, I invited friends over for a big dance party in my yard; Kendra was the DJ. I heard someone ask another guest. "Are you a dancer or a dreamer?" Even though my dream of starting over in Colorado no longer included my family, I had my dancing and dreaming friends. I felt grateful and blessed.

In March of 2014, I published my first book, *Living in the Shadow of the Too-Good Mother Archetype*. It took a lot of time: writing, editing, publishing, and marketing. I'm not sure I could have had been in a relationship while publishing a book and working full time.

Most importantly, I uncovered my saboteur: the deep unconscious result of that declaration I made standing outside of my mother's bedroom when I was eleven. *Never to love anyone as much as my mother had loved my father, because it would hurt too much.*

Had I been choosing men who couldn't stay because I was unable to truly open my heart and let them in? Had I, for the very same reason, been rejecting the men who might stay?

Around the time of my book release party I called Laurence to consult on a case. He was my go-to guy for addiction treatment. I still hadn't thought of dating him, as our relationship was strictly professional. He told me he had sold his business and his house and was moving to Denver.

I was in shock for him and his three major losses: wife, business, and home. I'd experienced many losses, so I understood the depth of those transitions. I wondered how he'd manage all three at once.

He told me he was taking a sabbatical. He wanted to write a book. He had cleared everything from his schedule except for one thing; my book release party. I was quite surprised that I ranked high enough to be the only thing he was going to make time for, other than writing his book. I was happy, and looked forward to sharing the evening with Laurence, my dancers, my dreamers, and me.

He never showed up. Honestly, I didn't even notice. It was a great night of celebrating a book that I had been writing for over eighteen years. We danced and laughed. I realized a few days later that he hadn't been there, and I just assumed his grief made it hard to do anything.

I had learned how to be happy alone, but I still longed for companionship. I wanted to come home and share my day with a partner again. I wanted to have dinner and watch television with a best friend. I was tired of being alone.

Facing my saboteur, I declared that I was *now* willing to love someone as much as my mother had loved my father. It was worth the risk. The depth of my mother's grief had defined the depth of her love. I realized it's impossible to have one without the other.

Shortly after I made my new declaration, I picked up a friend at the Denver airport. Mary Elizabeth Marlow, a spiritual teacher from Virginia, had come to Boulder to be a keynote speaker at my friend Billie Ortiz's Creativity Festival. I transported her to the hotel. The first thing Mary Elizabeth asked me was, "Are you seeing anyone?"

"What? Dating? Me? No. I've been spending time getting to know myself better."

She replied, "You need to put yourself out there. Let men know you're interested, or you'll keep yourself blocked off from love."

I was a bit taken aback that we were even having this conversation, and even more so that she had spoken so emphatically about the subject. I told her I had met a man at a swing dance class a few weeks earlier and another man recently at a lecture. She said I should ask them out.

Then I thought of Laurence. I hadn't thought about the possibility of dating him before, because it felt odd after all the years of having a strictly professional relationship and having known his wife.

"And," I added, surprising myself, "there's a man I know who lost his wife a year ago. I've always respected him, but it is probably too soon for him."

Mary Elizabeth quickly responded, "It's not too soon. Call him up. Ask him to lunch."

I told her that he was in France, but I would contact him as soon as he returned.

Break My Heart Open

When he returned from France, Laurence sent out an announcement about an *Open House* at his new psychotherapy office. I put it on my calendar and planned to follow through with Mary Elizabeth's advice. I was going to ask him to lunch. I was now on a mission.

I arrived a bit nervous. I brought him a candle in a gift bag, which he seemed to like. I talked to his other guests and mingled a bit. Laurence was busy making the rounds.

I found him when I was ready to say my goodbyes and to extend a quick invitation to lunch, when before I could finish, he asked, "You aren't leaving, are you? Sit. If you want to. Please, sit with me for a while."

I sat down in a chair to his left. He placed his arm around the top of my chair as he told me about his heart. "I've never experienced anything like this before. My heart has broken open to something much more than I've ever known. I can't quite explain it."

He had no idea I had been thinking about something more than a working relationship with him. Now I was really nervous. His heart. Why was he speaking so vulnerably about his heart? I had no idea what to say.

I remembered something I had heard after my divorce: *Break my heart open to a higher love.* That is what I shared with him. Then I ran, feeling scared, stupid and unsure of what I should have said or what he was trying to tell me.

A few days later, I sent him an e-mail with dates and times I could meet him for lunch. I hesitated for a minute but decided to add a Broncos game to the list of possibilities. I didn't have cable television at the time, so I would typically venture out to sports bars to watch the games.

He chose the Broncos.

Hi Laurence:

Congrats on the beautiful new digs!! So good to see you and share in the new developments in your life. I am getting ready to go to Vail for the weekend with girlfriends :)))

Here are some times I have for lunch:

Wed. Nov. 12 noon-2:00

Saturday Nov. 15 open anytime!

Sunday Nov 16—if you're a Broncos fan, I am always looking for someone to watch with—they play at 11:00!!

Tuesday Nov 18 or Friday Nov 21, brunch so that I can see clients by noon???

If these don't work, let me know what is best for you. Looking forward to it.

Have a great weekend,

Patti

Very cool idea. Let's watch the Broncos. Do you want to meet at Mile Hi, breakfast, hang time, game time? I know it makes it more of a day, and if it's over the top, I completely understand if you also want to limit to game time. Either way it will be fun to get together and celebrate all the good things both of us are doing.

Let me know,

Laurence

Hi Laurence:

Glad you like the idea. I was thinking about Mile Hi too if it was going to be a 2:00 game, but since the game starts at 11:00, it is probably best to just meet at Old Chicago a little before 11:00. I thought Westminster would be a good halfway place to meet. If I went to MH, I would have to get up at 5:30ish to make it to the 8:00 service....yikes...

Can't wait to spend time with you and catch up.

Patti

> Patti,
> Just a thought, but 5:30 is a little on the early side. Where is the Old Chicago in Westminster? I too am looking forward to spending time with you. See you on Sunday.
> Laurence

Two days later he called to see if I wanted to come to his house to watch the game instead. He said it would be quieter and he would fix us lunch. I agreed but told him I'd still owe him a lunch. He said not to worry. I asked if I could bring anything.

"Dessert," he replied.

I wondered, was this a date? He asked me to his house. I asked my friend Billie and she said, "Yes it's a date." I was really nervous. After many years of having a strictly professional relationship with him, the thought of being on a date seemed very weird.

I brought gluten-free brownies and acted as if it was a professional lunch.

We missed most of the game. We talked for hours.

He told me about his first marriage (which ended in divorce), and his thirty-three-year-old son from that relationship. I learned that he had had cancer right after his son was born. He told me the surgery included removing his intestines and then putting them back in. He said he had felt like the scarecrow in the Wizard of Oz when he lost his stuffing.

I also learned he had gotten sober at that time, and that he had stayed sober for thirty-three years.

I told him about my first marriage, my four children and my two grandchildren. I told him about my custody battles, my move to Colorado, losing Ken, and my financial challenges.

He told me how much he admired my courage and that he knew I had *lived on the skinny branches*. I had never heard that expression before, and I felt a tug on my heart. I had really been seen by this man. He knew me. Few people ever acknowledged the tremendous financial and emotional obstacles I'd dealt with.

But Laurence did.

He gave me a tour of his new apartment. A friend from church had helped him decorate. When I saw the print of a couple standing in front of the Eifel tower holding a red umbrella, I almost gasped. I was planning to be in France the following year. Maybe he would join me, I briefly thought to myself. He told me he had been advised by his decorator to hang the romantic print in his bedroom as a way to envision love coming back into his life.

Several times that day I tried to leave, but we just couldn't stop talking. It felt really nice to be with him. Our easy conversation went on for hours after the game, until we finally managed to say goodbye. I can't remember if the Broncos won or lost; or even who they played.

He walked me to my car and I put my hand in his arm because the parking lot was icy. I would have done that whether or not it had been a date. It was my fear of falling, not a gesture of romance. Still, I wasn't sure if he had thought it was a date, or not.

Speaking of falling, I think I was, but not on the ice. I drove home and decided to be open to what might be next. It was his turn to make a move, and I really hoped he would.

Clarity is Good

Two days after our Broncos lunch, I got a voicemail from Laurence.

Butterflies in my stomach for sure.

Several hours later, I called him back.

He answered.

"I'm, I'm, I'm not sure if this is okay. Please let me know if I am out of line.... But... I was wondering... would you like to go on a date with me?"

"Yes. I would love to!"

Then the words: *"Clarity is good,"* came out of my mouth!

He had no idea what I meant by that, but I was relieved. It was official. We were going on a real date.

That was now clear.

Our First Official Date

We made plans to go to dinner and a movie in Boulder. I gave him directions to my house and expected him to arrive at 5:00 p.m. On the way, he texted saying he was stuck in traffic. He apologized. I told him not to worry. That night I was so happy about our official first date, I didn't care.

Since he was one hour late, I asked if he wanted to walk around the little town of Niwot where I lived and eat at one of the restaurants there instead. I thought he might not want to get back into the car and drive into Boulder after being stuck in traffic for so long.

We walked around the little historic town that looks a bit like Mayberry RFD. I took him to my psychotherapy office that was across the street from my house. I showed him the little shops and the market, and then we had dinner at Treppedas, the Italian place in town.

He told me about his trip to France. I was planning to take a group there in a few months and was very interested in hearing his story, especially about the Labyrinth in Chartres Cathedral. He showed me pictures. It felt so easy with him, like being home.

I mentioned that the Powder Keg Brewery had music on Friday nights, and asked if he was okay with going there since he was in recovery. He quickly answered that he'd like to go. It didn't bother him at all to be around alcohol. He'd been sober for so long that it wasn't a craving anymore.

We talked and talked and talked some more. I asked if *Freedom* was his given last name. He told me his real name was actually Larry Ratcliff. He shared the story about a nun who had come to the treatment center where he had gotten sober. She wrote the word *FREEDOM* on the board as she told a profound and moving story. He later decided to make that his name.

I mentioned the movies *Before Sunrise* and *Before Sunset* since they were filmed in Europe and we'd been talking about his France trip. He told me that Suzan had loved those movies, but he never really was that interested in them. He said he hadn't seen the second one at all.

When I told him I had the movie, he asked if we could go back to my house and watch it.

We sat together on the sofa, his arm around me. I leaned my head on his shoulder while he stroked my hair. Not only was I happy about that, I was delighted to be watching one of my favorite movies with him.

These films starring Ethan Hawke are about a couple who meet on a train in Europe. Each movie is about one twenty-four-hour period of time. They meet again, ten years later, in the second one.

I enjoy the conversations and the way the story of a day goes.

I wondered how our story might go.

Seeing Him Again

We agreed we had had fun, and then shared a kiss on the cheek goodbye.

I wanted to wait for him to call me, but I couldn't. The next day I texted him to see if he was going to church on Sunday. He said he was and would save me a seat.

We sat with his friend, Debra.

He invited me to walk the labyrinth later that day, and afterwards have dinner with Debra and Larry. Of course, I said yes.

During dinner, Laurence asked me out on official dates number two and three. We made plans to go to a University of Colorado football game when he returned from visiting his sister for Thanksgiving. The following week we planned to see his friend Cheryl Wheeler in concert, at Swallow Hill in Denver.

I was very happy to be officially dating Laurence Freedom.

That day at Mile Hi Church, I remembered many days I had spent there alone, seeking comfort from loss and pain. My life had been full of endings: custody battles, lost loves, lost jobs, and endless worries about money. Mile Hi gave me solace. I went there to pray. We both called Mile Hi Church our spiritual home. I was very grateful that we could now share this part of our lives together.

Lost in the Labyrinth

Laurence was a practitioner at Mile Hi Church. Practitioners are somewhat like deacons in the Catholic Church. They go through many years of training and practice to be able to function in service and prayer for members of the congregation.

Laurence loved to pray for people. He would stop by the prayer and guidance center after church, anxious to pick up prayer requests that had been left by congregants on Sunday. He had an effervescent light around him, and people often felt healing energy just by being in his presence.

Walking a labyrinth is a meditation practice that I discovered many years ago. The maze-like winding path leads you around in a circle. There are times when you think you're close to the center, and then a few steps later you're back on the outer edge. It's a walk of faith and patience. For me, it's a mindfulness practice that brings me clarity and peace, as I walk and listen to my inner guidance.

Jean Shinoda Bolen, in her book *Crossing to Avalon*, wrote about her experience of walking the labyrinth in the Chartres Cathedral in France: "We find what really matters to us and can reach the core or center of meaning in ourselves, which is the center of the labyrinth, and then we have the task of integrating this into what we do with our lives when we emerge." (p.163)

The first Sunday that we met for church happened to be a day when Mile Hi had a labyrinth set up for congregants to walk. As we walked it together, I had a labyrinth experience like never before! We ambled around on the path passing each other, smiling and looking into each other's eyes. At one point, we both laughed out loud as this flirtatious circle dance continued around and around again.

Then it happened. We stepped off our paths and we were lost. Lost in the labyrinth. Kind of hard to do, but we did it. I have no idea what Laurence was feeling that day, but I knew I was falling in love. Even though we were off the path, we were definitely on the right track back to each other.

Dance Me to the End of Love

The days that followed were pure bliss. Since we lived thirty-plus miles apart, we only saw each other on the weekends and an occasional weeknight. I anxiously looked forward to each and every date.

Arriving at his apartment, I was greeted by Jasper, his adorable Aussie-Shepherd mix dog. Leonard Cohen was frequently playing on Pandora. Even though I had never been a big Cohen fan, I was very turned on by the sultry music playing in the background as this man prepared me a meal. I knew I wanted to be with him. I knew he was going to be my new man, different from all of the rest.

When I told him that it had been six years since I had been with anyone, he was worried. We had a long talk about it. He assumed I wanted a commitment. He wasn't sure what he wanted. I told him it was too soon for us to make a commitment, and not to worry.

I loved the sincerity and integrity in his eyes as we talked. I knew he was safe. *Do no harm* he would say, from his commitment to AA. I was confident we would always be kind and respectful to each other. He was well worth the consequences of falling. No matter what happened.

In the past I'd had an eight-date rule when dating. There were the men who couldn't wait for eight dates before having sex: *not* worth it. Then there were the ones who were willing but tried to speed things up by asking if phone calls counted as a date. Or they'd schedule frequent dates to arrive at the winning number *ASAP*. Comical, actually. I had known Laurence for so long that he got a pass on our fourth date.

He was worried about hurting me, and I was worried that I might go back into my old pattern of disposing of good guys. I didn't want to hurt him after all his loss, either. He didn't want to hurt me knowing I had lost my father at a young age and had been alone for so long.

I told him we were both codependent and needed to decide for ourselves what we each wanted. I'm happy about the choice we made that night.

We talked. We laughed. We made love. We fell in love. The day after we first made love, Laurence wrote me a poem called *I Love Your Blue Eyes*. In the past I would have thought it was too much. With Laurence it felt right and wonderful.

The first year we were together was nothing short of wonderful. We went on eight trips in less than twelve months: Hawaii for New Year's Eve; Kansas for a wedding in February; California for my daughter's college graduation in May; Virginia Beach for the Fourth of July; Black Hills, South Dakota to visit the Crazy Horse Memorial; The Big Barn Dance in Taos; Nashville in October, and then a few days later, a Disneyland family reunion and birthday party; and Tucson for Thanksgiving, stopping in Santa Fe on the way there to buy a special ring.

When we traveled, he always got us coffee first thing in the morning. He drank his with cream and no sugar; I often sent him back to get me more sugar. Eventually he learned, and he began bringing large handfuls of sugar back to our room.

We were good travelers together.

It was all so easy and fun.

To Make You Feel My Love

One night while we were in Laurence's living room, the Bob Dylan song "To Make You Feel My Love" sung by Adele, came on Pandora. I asked Laurence to dance with me, and I softly sang in his ear. I knew he'd been through a lot of loss and needed time to be sure about us. The lyrics spoke to my willingness to wait for him and love him no matter what.

It became our song. Every time we heard it, we would smile and hold each other close.

We had a lot of songs.

We would lay in bed. morning and night, sharing songs from YouTube and our playlists. "Secret Garden" by Bruce Springsteen was one of his favorites. He said the lyrics expressed the way he felt about the beauty and mystery of a woman. He wanted me to understand how profound his love was for me. He played many Leonard Cohen songs, including "I'm Your Man."

I shared a song with him that I had heard at a music festival in Taos, sung by Chuck Cannon and his wife Lori White, called "I Love the Way You Love Me." And one morning I bravely shared the song "I Choose You" by Sara Bareilles. It's about making a commitment to a relationship. I was a bit worried it was too much too fast, but I did it anyway. He didn't seem to mind. I had no doubt that he was the one for me. He was everything I'd waited for and more.

I shared with him the insights I'd gained from being single for so long. I told him how I'd stood outside my mother's bedroom door that night when I was eleven years old while she was wailing in her grief, and how I declared that *I* would never love anyone that much. Then I explained to him how my six years of introspective self-discovery had uncovered my saboteur. I wanted our relationship to be different from any I'd had before.

Another song we both loved to share together was by a local artist Rebecca Folsom, called "The Back of My Heart." It goes like this: *"There are no words for some kinds of love, only revealed in a look or a touch. I love you, love you, back from the start. I love you, love you, back, from the back of my heart."*

He often told me he wasn't going anywhere. He wanted to protect and care for me knowing I'd lost my father at such a young age. He wanted to be my man.

A few months into dating, Laurence had a reading with Elisa, a spiritual medium. His deceased wife Suzan came through, and said she had sent me to Laurence.

Since losing my father, I'd come to believe in messages from the other side. However, I didn't expect *that* kind of a message! It hit me hard. I believed it was true. But I wasn't sure what to do with the information, other than chalk it up as a confirmation we were meant to be together.

It stunned me. I remember going to the bank that day and to a meeting that night. Several people asked me if I was okay, so I must've had some crazed look on my face.

It was a bit crazy after all.

Beautiful Kauai

Laurence had met Debra and Larry through our friend Junia, who leads spiritual tours around the world. Debra and Larry alternate spending time in their homes in Colorado and Kauai throughout the year.

Six months after Suzan's death, Laurence had gone to Kauai and stayed with Debra and Larry. He took Suzan's ashes back to the place where they had been married and said goodbye. He threw his wedding ring into the ocean with the ashes. He had lost Suzan's ring, and didn't want his without hers. Later, however, he found her ring, and regretted tossing his into the Pacific Ocean.

A few weeks into dating Laurence, he decided to go back to Kauai. He told Debra that he wanted to bring me. She encouraged him to sign up for an Alaskan Air credit card where he could have a buddy fly for free.

He asked me to go, with the familiar hesitation he had when he asked me out on our first date, "I'm not sure if this is appropriate. Let me know how you feel. But I was talking to Debra about this, and I was wondering if you might want to go to Kauai with me on New Year's Eve."

Silence on my end.

Of course, I wanted to go.

I was mostly concerned that I couldn't financially contribute to the trip. I had recently made a decision to rebuild my psychotherapy practice after having closed it to take a job with the school district a few years prior. Money was very tight; *very, very* tight. He told me not to worry. He would get the buddy pass from Alaskan Air and cover everything.

I learned during our time together that I was not familiar, nor comfortable with receiving. That was one of those times. Could I accept this big-ticket item?

Yes.

Magic. The whole week. We had *two* New Year's Eve midnight

kisses since we changed time zones while in flight.

We had a long layover in Seattle, where Laurence's brother Ed and his partner live. He wanted to get together with them during the eight hours we had to kill. I, too, had a friend who lived there with his partner. I asked Laurence if we could meet with Nick as well. He agreed. Little did we know that Nick was in a choir with Ed's partner, Joe. What a fun time we all had with introductions, synchronicities, coffee, and conversation.

After arriving in Kauai, we spent our days and nights on the beach. We were typical tourists. He took me to a Luau. He bought me a T-shirt and other souvenirs, including coffee that was made there. He loved the song *Beautiful Kauai* and would sing it and dance with me every time we heard it.

Prior to our trip, I didn't know how much Laurence enjoyed the ocean. He was a Colorado native. I had grown up in Virginia Beach and had spent most of my summers swimming in the ocean and soaking up the sun, until my move to Colorado. I was pleasantly surprised as we lay on the Hawaiian beach and swam in the ocean, body surfing and kissing in between. He liked the beach as much as me.

One day we walked across the golf course near Larry and Debra's house. We stopped and stood hand in hand as the moon was rising on one side and the sun was setting on the other. I led him around in a swirling circle dance. We laughed and hugged and kissed. He talked frequently about how magical that night was, as if the Universe had lined up just for us.

According to an astrology reading we had a few months later, our stars certainly did line up! He had an Aries sun and a Cancer moon. I have a Cancer sun and an Aries moon. We were a pair of opposites. Aries people are about fire and determination. Cancers are about love and family. We both definitely held those qualities. We complimented each other perfectly.

The full Hawaii moon came into our window at night. We sometimes woke up and made love in its soft light. It was something we had come to do quite frequently. Magic.

Even though I loved being there with him, I still felt a bit strange.

I knew it was the place where he had married Suzan.
I wondered what it felt like to him to have me there.
I told him I wanted us to have a new special place.
We agreed it was probably going to be France.

Kansas

In February, his cousin was getting married in Kansas, where Laurence had many relatives. His sister and her husband planned to attend. He asked me if I wanted to go, offering to cover all expenses. Again, I said yes.

His sister and her husband picked us up late one night at the airport. He told me I would like his sister because she was very easygoing. It was true. We stayed with his cousin in her very large house, I met many more cousins. The whole family embraced me and welcomed me in.

In less than three months I had met both of his siblings, and lots of other cousins!

The Fool's Journey

In April, Laurence went to Brazil with a group from Mile Hi Church. While I was taking him to the airport, he shared with me a few of his dreams. A recurring image was him standing on a balcony or a ledge. It made me think of *The Fool* in the Tarot.

I shared with him what *The Fool* means to me. The first card in the deck, known as zero, represents the beginning of a journey. *The Fool* is jumping off a cliff with just a small duffle bag and a little dog. Trust and chance.

Laurence's trip to Brazil was a fool's journey. He had planned the trip to help him heal his grief. Instead the journey became one of endings and beginnings.

Before he departed, we had started a conversation about living together.

While he was traveling, I painted an image of *The Fool* on a large canvas as his birthday gift. Coincidentally, he was going to be gone twenty-two days, the same number of days as there are in the major arcana of the Tarot. So, in addition to the painting, each day of his trip I wrote him a hand-written letter with a corresponding tarot card, and then placed each one in a box that I decorated by hand. I used a tarot card each day as a way to describe his fool's journey and our time apart. When he returned, I gave him the painting and the box of letters to celebrate his sixty-first birthday and his homecoming.

He was excited to share his stories of Brazil with me, but he was especially enthusiastic about a vision he had had on the trip related to creating a healing center for people with codependency issues.

We immediately began to plan how we could create that vision together.

We weren't sure how it would happen, but we trusted the process.

As does *The Fool!*

Confusion Hill

In May we decided to travel to northern California to celebrate my youngest daughter's college graduation and her twenty-ninth birthday. There Laurence would meet my daughter, my three-year-old grandson, and my youngest son.

We flew into San Francisco and drove six hours north to where my daughter lives. On the way we saw a sign for *Confusion Hill*. We couldn't resist pulling over.

Confusion Hill sits on a vortex that defies gravity. We walked through a crooked little house where we were unable to stand up straight. Gravity pulled us to one side. Laurence especially loved the little rail where golf balls roll up instead of down.

Back on the road, we laughed and shared our thoughts about how this was a metaphor for relationships.

Laurence and I had been talking about writing a book about relationship. I thought *Confusion Hill* would make a great chapter title.

He told me he had some trepidation about us writing a book together. He was worried I might get frustrated with him. He felt inadequate since I was a published author. I told him I might, but that would be okay. Part of the process.

I had always seen Laurence as so self-confident. This was the first time he had shared any insecurity or self-doubt.

Confused at *Confusion Hill.*

Laurence Freedom worried about not being good enough? News to me!

When we returned home, he wrote this blog:

This past weekend, my partner Patti and I traveled up the Northern California coast to be with two of her children and to celebrate her youngest daughter's birthday and college graduation. As we drove up Route 101 we came across an off-road attraction called Confusion Hill.

Confusion Hill is a magnetic vortex where normal laws of gravity are backwards. Water runs uphill, and you can roll a golf ball down a narrow shoot, and it will roll right back, defying the laws of gravity. Standing in the house of confusion, you cannot help but feel disorientated, and walking becomes challenging as you feel your body being pulled upward.

Many relationships are based upon dependency, not love, which causes confusion. Is it love or is it dependency? In the addiction field we are learning more and more about dependency relationships and the dynamics of how these relationships look and how they operate. On one end of the spectrum you have relationships that are driven by the need to be attached or merged, no matter what the cost. These relationships normally entail sacrificing or losing a sense of self. It is common that people who have this dependency pattern will merge with someone on the other end of the spectrum who is unavailable to be close and intimate in a relationship. Many times, these people are caught up in other addictions: alcohol, drugs, sex, work, food, or money for example.

The one common missing element in all dependency relationships is self-love. Sacrificing and losing oneself in a relationship is not love. Looking for love in all the wrong places, with all the wrong people, is not love. Chasing the intensity of the high with a new relationship or posting the sexual conquest on a headboard is not love. Love starts with self, yet for many, self-love is missing.

The healing process from dependency relationships begins with counting, valuing, and loving yourself. It is about falling in love with you, not from a narcissistic ego-driven frenzy needing reassurance and self-gratification, but from the place of how a parent sees a child and all the wonder that exists within their soul.

Self-love comes from healing the wounds of the past where love was absent or other forms of abuse were injected into the early years of growing up as a child. Self-love is the key to a healthy, vibrant, flourishing relationship. To truly love someone, you must possess that love for yourself first. This is not confusing, but it does entail a lot of work to break the pattern of dependency relationships. I invite you to step off confusion hill and engage in practices of self-love to enrich your life and all those around you.

Little did I know then, but this was the *real* beginning of our relationship. We began to look at our own confusion. Was this love, or dependency, or maybe a little of both? Either way, we were having fun finding out. He was my very best friend.

Mr. Laurence

Laurence told me he was happy that I have four children. He wasn't sure if his son was going to have children, and he liked the idea of being a grandfather to mine. I had never dated anyone that excited about my children and grandchildren. *Who does that?* I thought. Laurence.

I was delighted.

We spent the Fourth of July and my fifty-seventh birthday in Virginia Beach. There he met my two older children, their significant others, and my two-year-old granddaughter. He was looking forward to the visit because he had heard about the movie *Frozen* from his four-year-old second cousin, and he had been anticipating watching it with my granddaughter.

The two of them sat side by side on the sofa and watched the entire movie. A few days later my daughter sent me a stick figure picture her daughter had drawn in school, titled *My Family*. In it she had labeled the people in the drawing: *Mom, Dad, Grandma,* and *Mr. Laurence.* He had obviously made an impression.

We stayed with my former college roommate Sabina and her husband in their condo on the beach. We walked to the ocean for fireworks on the Fourth and returned home to the balcony overlooking all the cars trying to get through the traffic jams after the celebration. Laurence and Byron smoked a cigar. Laurence said that smoking a cigar was the one guilty pleasure he had left after getting sober so long ago.

I was excited to show Laurence the Association for Research and Enlightenment (ARE), founded by the late Edgar Cayce. It now houses a bookstore, library, meditation room, spa, labyrinth, and restaurant. Cayce was known as the *Sleeping Prophet.* He would do life readings for people and intuit natural methods of healing. Many of his treatments still exist today, such as castor oil packs placed on the body for healing.

We went up to the meditation room on the top floor that overlooked the Atlantic Ocean. We sat in silence for about thirty minutes.

Then we went outside and walked the labyrinth, smiling at the memory of the first time we had been *lost on the path*.

Laurence signed us up for a membership, so that we could look through the Cayce health remedies for the plantar fasciitis I had been suffering with. He always wanted to help and heal. *Everyone.*

As in Hawaii, we swam in the ocean and lay on the beach. Summer was our favorite season. Another thing we had in common.

That summer there had been several shark attacks at that beach. My family was sure to warn us about it. Laurence told everyone that he wasn't afraid of the sharks. I laughed because when we were swimming in the ocean, it was the jellyfish he was deathly afraid of! I had fun teasing him about that.

We drove down to Nags Head, North Carolina on my birthday. After a day of playing on the beach, we searched for the perfect place to eat crabs. I had told Laurence about my fond childhood memories of bringing in the crab pots, and then cracking them for hours.

We found a buffet that had thirty types of crabs from all over, as well as many other kinds of seafood. It was messy, with buckets on the tables for the shells. Laurence was happy I had my crab, but I think he would have preferred us getting dressed up and going out for some romantic fine dining.

Even though he loved the ocean, he had grown up in Colorado. He wasn't used to crab shells flying all over the table. To me, it felt like home.

Ladybugs—Lots of Them!

When our astrologer charted our compatibility, she started with individual readings for each of us. In mine, Cynthia told me that my life's purpose was to heal the Sacred Feminine. I had been working with women for years, and especially called to the Mary Magdalene archetype as a way to illustrate the historical suppression of the feminine.

The astrologer was exactly right about my life's work.

Laurence had a lot of respect for women and felt my task of healing the wounds of the feminine was very important. When I shared the reading with him, he said, "I want to help you. I don't want you to have to do it all alone anymore."

I had never had much help with anything in my life. Losing my dad, not having a very involved husband, and then being divorced left me mostly doing everything on my own. One lesson I learned from being with Laurence was how to receive. I was grateful he wanted to be my man. I could breathe a bit more easily knowing I was no longer on my own.

As we talked about how he might help me, a ladybug crawled across my kitchen counter. I shouted, "Oh, my God... Oh, my god... Oh, my god!"

Laurence responded, "What is it? Are you all right?"

I then told him this ladybug story.

Shortly after my mother died in 2008, a ladybug landed on a tightly closed window in my old school building office. I watched the little red bug slowly wander around. I wondered how it could have landed directly in front of me. The windows were nailed shut on the third floor a long way from the outside world.

After a few minutes of child-like reverence, I thought about my mother. Of course, she would have said hello that way.

A few weeks later I attended a workshop with Dr. Patty Luckenbach from Mile Hi Church. Dr. Patty has a deep connection to Mother Earth and Native American spirituality. When I told Patty about the ladybug, she confirmed my suspicion by saying, "That was your mother."

Later, I discovered that some people believe ladybugs are good luck. If you set one free, it brings you back your soulmate. From then on, every time I saw a ladybug, I set it free.

When the ladybug showed up on my kitchen counter that day, I knew Laurence was my soulmate. It was confirmed. He was the one I had been waiting for all these years.

The first time I visited Laurence's home, I noticed a ladybug welcome mat on his doorstep. I smiled and wondered if my mom was meddling. Today, the ladybug doormat sits on my backdoor step as a daily reminder of our ladybug love affair.

Laurence frequently bought me ladybug things. Lots of them! Little ceramic ladybugs, a ladybug finger puppet, ladybug salt and pepper shakers, a ladybug chocolate that I will never eat, and ladybug socks, only to name just a few. Every morning he said, "Good morning, my Ladybug," and every night, "Good night, my Ladybug."

Moving In

Laurence and I moved fast in the direction of living together. Prior to moving in, we packed weekend bags and drove fifty-five minutes each way, spending most weekends at either his place or mine.

Laurence had sold his marital home the previous year and was renting an apartment in Lakewood. His lease was running out that summer, and I was having a hard time paying all my bills while also rebuilding my psychotherapy practice. Since I owned my house and loved my little town of Niwot, Laurence decided he would make the drive into work from my house and we would give up the weekend trips back and forth.

In between our May and July trips to meet my children, we were packing and planning our life together. On Memorial Day weekend, we each put some of each of our things in storage, to make more room for what Laurence wanted to bring to help him feel at home.

Even though I was very sure about our relationship, it was a huge change for both of us. I hoped he wasn't moving in quickly with me as a way to avoid some unresolved grief over losing his wife. Was I just a drug to numb his pain? Confusion Hill!

He had dated another woman a few months after Suzan died. She wasn't interested in a serious relationship with him at the time. That's when I had come into the picture. He had gone from his first marriage straight into a relationship with Suzan and then started dating very shortly after Suzan died.

Our conversation at Confusion Hill kicked off my questioning. Was he really with me because he felt the same love as I did for him, or was he afraid of being alone? I wanted him to be sure.

Another profound thing I learned in my first graduate class in 1989 was the stages of relationships. The first three to six months of a relationship are often ruled by *happy hormones,* when the couple experiences what feels like a high. After that, the rose-colored glasses come off, and the real work begins. We then have to ask ourselves, "Is this person worth the commitment and effort of a relationship?" This is when a lot of people run away. That's the nature of sex/love addiction. Getting the initial high of falling in love is something we all crave, but the truth is it doesn't last.

Romantic love is the way we play out our projections, or the unrecognized parts of ourselves onto others. We don't typically pay attention to the deeper meaning of romantic love when we get swept away into the rush of the newness of a relationship. Yet, ultimately, it all shows up as a way to essentially help us grow.

How, then, do we tell the difference between healthy partnership and the addictive high? Regardless, our projections onto the other person in the attraction phase are there to help us learn about ourselves. It's up to us to dig deeper into those places; it's there we decide whether or not we can tolerate our own flaws as well as our partner's.

Then the real work begins.

Laurence was committed to his sobriety and had not touched a drop of alcohol for thirty-five years. I was so proud of him for that. I know many who struggle with addiction, and the relapse rate is very high. Staying sober is hard work. Laurence was devoted to that path.

After his wife died, he found himself lost in loneliness and longing. He wanted to be with someone; however, he questioned whether or not his longing was an addiction he hadn't yet addressed.

I knew he was the right man for me, and I was willing to move fully into a relationship with him. Still, I wanted him to be as sure about me as I was about him. I had been alone a long time and didn't feel the need to be with someone specifically from the fear of being alone.

Laurence had clearly stated that he was a recovering codependent, afraid of being alone. He also told me he had been attending twelve-step meetings for sex and love addiction. I never saw him as a sex addict. He didn't cheat on Suzan, and he didn't watch porn. It was more the love part; he hated being alone; he numbed his pain by caretaking others.

Even though we'd talked a lot about our motivations for being together, and we both agreed it was a healthy choice, I sometimes wondered. Was he really in love with me, or was I another addiction?

One night I posed the question of whether or not ninety days without a relationship might be helpful for him, and us. Familiar with the journey of sobriety, I knew that when someone makes a decision to get sober, ninety twelve-step meetings in ninety days are recommended, in addition to no intimate relationships. I thought ninety days alone might help him with his grief over Suzan, and also help us to be sure I wasn't just another addiction. I told him he was the addiction expert, and he would know better than I. However, I felt we should address the idea together as we were moving forward in our commitment to each other.

He said I made some good points, and he would sleep on it.

I worried all night that he might take me up on the ninety days of separation. I didn't *want* to be without him *at all*. I had waited all my life for a man like this, and I had been single for six years prior. Still, I wanted to be sure we were together for the right reasons. I was willing to sacrifice three months of our time together to be sure he was sure about us.

When he called the next morning, he said he'd thought about what I said, and he was sure that being in a relationship with me was the right thing. He felt we would be okay moving forward as planned. I was relieved and happy.

Still, the night before we rented the U-Haul on Memorial Day weekend to move our things into storage, I had a panic attack. I can be anxious at times, but I don't think I'd ever before had a full-blown panic attack like that one. I couldn't breathe. I couldn't sleep. I just kept wondering if we were making a big mistake.

I didn't want to have him move into my house and then have to ask him to leave if it didn't work out. I had always left the good guys. I didn't want to do that to him. I didn't want to hurt him. I didn't want to relive what it felt like to leave my marriage.

I knew this was the beginning of a big commitment.

Should we wait?

We talked and talked and talked about it. He eased my fears. He told me people grow together in a relationship. He assured me it would be fine. He also told me it was up to me. I told him that I wanted to be with him more than anything, but I was scared.

By the morning I felt better and ready to get the truck. I was glad Laurence and I could talk so openly about everything.

We actually had fun that day sorting and moving and planning the next steps for us.

Our House is a Very, Very, Very Fine House

By the end of July, we were all settled into my house—our house. We loved being together without the long weekend drive. It was nice to have him in my arms every night and to spend my mornings with him. Living with Laurence was easy. He was kind, gentle, warm, and affectionate.

Codependents make the best caretakers. I was one, too. Our relationship was one big giving fest. Who could do more for the other? Not that we were competing or complaining, we just liked taking care of each other. I finally had met my match.

We loved doing projects together. He liked building things and feeling a sense of accomplishment. We painted. We built shelves and an entertainment center. We organized the garage and the yard and spent many weekends at Home Depot and Lowes.

I felt so grateful to be sharing my day-to-day life with him. It was such a new and wonderful way of being in a relationship for me. When I told him how much I appreciated him, he responded, "That's partnership Patti, *partnership,* that's how it works." Laurence taught me the value of relationship, and how to honor each individual's role in the lovely dance.

His dog Jasper, and my two cats Jack and Mogley, lounged in the yard. We spent almost every summer night having dinner on the patio under my red umbrella, just like the lovers under the red umbrella in the print he had on his bedroom wall.

We took many walks with Jasper. We talked about the animals and birds we saw. They all had meaning to us. When we got back home, we sat on my porch swing and looked them up in a book called *Animal Speak* by Ted Andrews. Laurence compared himself to a red-tailed hawk: he liked to soar above the worldly demands.

I loved his spirituality and his kindness.

I loved our walks and talks and days together.

When we were having our yard sale to get rid of some extra stuff after he moved in, a man mentioned he was on his way to *Santiago's,* a local Mexican restaurant. It piqued Laurence's attention, as he was always on a quest for the best chiles rellenos. It became his favorite place to dine. If I ever wondered where he might want to go, *Santiago's* was a sure bet, breakfast, lunch, or dinner.

Every night as we lay in bed, he listed all the things we had done that day. It was his gratitude practice. For someone who would often forget things, I was impressed with every little detail he would relay. Starting with our morning coffee and including every single facet of the day until we crawled into bed that night. He would always ask me if I could think of anything else. He had usually covered it all, including some things I had already forgotten!

This evening ritual touched my heart so much that some nights I would eagerly remind him, saying, *"Do our day."* I'd lay with my head on his chest, his arm around me, and I'd listen intently with such gratitude for this incredible man and our precious time together.

Crazy Horse

In August we packed up the dog and headed to the Black Hills.

Early in our relationship, Laurence had showed me a one-thousand-page manuscript that his friend, Ed Heisel, had written entitled *Mystic Warrior: Crazy Horse*. Ed died a few months after Suzan. Years before Ed passed away, he had asked Laurence to help him get the book published.

Crazy Horse was a Lakota warrior who honored the Native American way of life. He fought with Sitting Bull in the American-Indian Wars and was instrumental in beating Custer at the Battle of the Little Bighorn. After surrendering to federal troops in 1877, he was killed to prevent his suspected potential for escape.

I wanted to know more about Crazy Horse, so I asked Laurence to take me to South Dakota. I had never been there before and had no idea what to expect. I didn't realize there was such a contrast of commercialized vacation and children's activities, sitting on and close to the sacred Native American land. I felt a strange ambivalence. I was happy that children could come and play there at the theme parks, but I was saddened that some of the spiritual essence of the native people had been massacred.

As we were trying to find our campground, we got a bit turned around and stopped at Old McDonald Petting Farm to reroute. As Laurence took Jasper for a short walk, we noticed several goats walking back and forth high up on a tight-wire in front of the entrance. I videoed the goats for a few minutes on my phone, and after the trip Laurence loved showing it to all of our friends. He got a such a big kick out of the *tight-rope goat walk!*

The next day our first stop was the Crazy Horse Memorial. The Lakota people are building it without any funding from the government. They want to be sure it won't be influenced by anyone outside of their people. It is taking quite a while to build and will continue to be many years in the making.

I was grateful to have the chance to share in this place with Laurence. I knew how dear it was to his heart. Crazy Horse is an important archetype, a clear way to imagine a peaceful warrior. We could certainly use more of those. Men and women who fight for integrity, justice, and the human spirit. Ed's book highlights how this man was a mystic warrior teaching spiritual truths. I understood why Laurence wanted to get the book published. It has a valuable message for us today.

I have a copy of the manuscript, and hope to one day get it published.

We also went to Mount Rushmore.

It was interesting to be there and see it up close.

As always, we had a great time together.

The Big Barn Dance

In September, we headed to Taos, New Mexico for the Big Barn Dance. It had been a tradition of mine for the previous eight years. I was happy Laurence liked Texas-Americana music and was willing to go with me this time.

We stayed in the hotel where Georgia O-Keefe often came to paint. I love the adobe; the color; and the art in New Mexico. Laurence did, too. Was this man too good to be true? We had so much in common.

He was always clear about his likes and dislikes. If he didn't like something, he'd say, "That's not mine."

I was so happy we could share the things we both enjoyed, together.

First, the labyrinth and our similar spiritual practice, then swimming in the ocean, and now dancing in the southwest. All my favorite things side-by-side my beloved. No longer alone. I liked it, and I loved him.

At the Big Barn Dance there were two large dance floors, set up with people two-stepping and waltzing all weekend long. I love all types of dance. Since I'd been single for so long, I typically line-danced or danced solo with my *Planet Motion* friends. I had done some partner dancing through the years, but I wasn't a good follower and didn't have much practice.

But I have rhythm.

Laurence, on the other hand, had *no* rhythm. I led him around the dance floor, whispering "Slow, slow, quick, quick," the steps I knew for two-step dancing. He followed my lead. He smiled in terror of losing the beat. Precious.

On Saturday morning, we went to St. Francis of Assisi Church in Taos. Laurence was fascinated by *The Shadow of the Cross*, a painting by 18th-century artist Henri Ault, which was kept locked in a large closet. It's a portrait of Jesus in Galilee. When the pastor turns off the lights, a cross appears over Jesus' shoulder, and sometimes seems to be moving. Laurence loved telling our friends about this mystery. He was fascinated by it.

While we were in Taos we were fortunate to meet Joan Borysenko, a well-known author and teacher, and her husband Gordon. I had been reading Joan's books on spirituality and mindfulness for years. I contacted Joan prior to our trip to NM, because Laurence and I had been brainstorming who might be able to help us develop our vision of a healing center for codependency.

We had learned that Gold Lake Mountain Resort in the mountains of Colorado had just gone on the market. It had been a treatment center for young men for the past five years. Before that, it had been a spa, a resort, an event center, and a few other things. Since Joan and her husband had lived near there for many years, I thought it might be a good connection to make. It was.

Joan and Gordon had moved to Santé Fe a few years prior. They just so happened to be going to the Big Barn Dance that weekend. We met them at the show and planned to meet for breakfast on Sunday. Gordon, coincidentally, had plans to talk with one of the owners of the Gold Lake property the following Monday. He said he would be happy to make an introduction for us.

Serendipity at its best.

It was a delight to meet them both.

A kismet connection.

Another magical adventure with my *Freedom*.

Nashville

After Gordon put us in touch with the owners of Gold Lake, we were gifted the use of the property for a visioning retreat. As part of our planning, we invited Dr. Patty to lunch so that we could discuss her offering a Lakota ceremony during the weekend retreat.

When we walked out of the restaurant after lunch that day, we surprisingly looked up and saw Joan and Gordon. We were all a bit stunned at the long odds of them being in Denver at the same restaurant, at the same time, on that day. It was no accident, we all concurred.

Joan introduced us to her friend Lee McCormick and invited us to come back inside and have dessert with them. It was delightful to spend more time together after having just met Joan and Gordon in Taos a few weeks prior.

Lee and Laurence had much in common. They talked non-stop about their work in addiction treatment and recovery. Lee owns and operates the Integrative Life Center in Nashville, TN. I was impressed by the nature of Lee's philosophy. He treats the whole person like a human being, and not just as a disease. I liked him from the minute we met. Kindred spirits.

After we conversed a while, Lee asked, "Do you two want to come to Nashville next week?" He jokingly said his assistant wouldn't be happy about the last-minute addition to his scheduled group tour but assured us that it would be all right.

We rearranged our client schedules and headed to Nashville. We met Lee's team of counselors and healers. We were invited to participate in meditations, healing rituals, and we even walked a labyrinth!

After the others in the group left, we stayed an extra night in Nashville to take in the music scene. I took a photo of Laurence next to Leonard Cohen at the Country Music Hall of Fame. He was such a big fan. As always, we had a lot of fun. At the end of the night, we split a caramel apple from the local five and dime.

Laurence loved that.

Disneyland

The week after Nashville, we went to Los Angeles to celebrate Laurence's niece's third birthday at Disneyland. Laurence's sister rented a house for the family for the week.

Laurence loved his family.

He often talked about his nephew John with high esteem. John met Vanessa when he moved to Brazil from his New England hometown, many years ago. Laurence had visited both of them when he journeyed to Brazil to see John of God. Laurence enjoyed meeting Vanessa's family and sharing in the Brazilian meals and traditions.

I got to meet them in California. We all knew John planned to ask Vanessa to marry him, but we were keeping it a secret until he popped the question. We all waited anxiously to celebrate. We were extremely excited when she finally showed us the ring.

I told Laurence about the Disneyland trip that my family and I had taken shortly after I turned twelve, the same year that my father died. My dad had promised me that I could visit my brother, his wife, and new baby in Arizona that year. My mother held a strong value about keeping promises, so she was sure to follow-through on my father's word. Part of the vacation included a long drive from Arizona to California.

As a child, I remember arriving in Disneyland and seeing the huge Mickey Mouse topiary at the entrance to the park. It seemed massive to me. But I wasn't impressed. Not much impressed me after my father died. He was a hard act to follow.

Yet, my family wanted me to be happy.

Laurence was devoted to me and knew the loss of my father had left some deep scars. Since he was the man I was doing a new type of relationship with after I declared my willingness to love, we both viewed this trip to Disneyland as another layer of my healing.

We rode the rides and got ice cream and then called it a day before the fireworks. I was disappointed because fireworks are one of my favorite things, but luckily when we arrived at the house, we could see them in the distance from the hot tub.

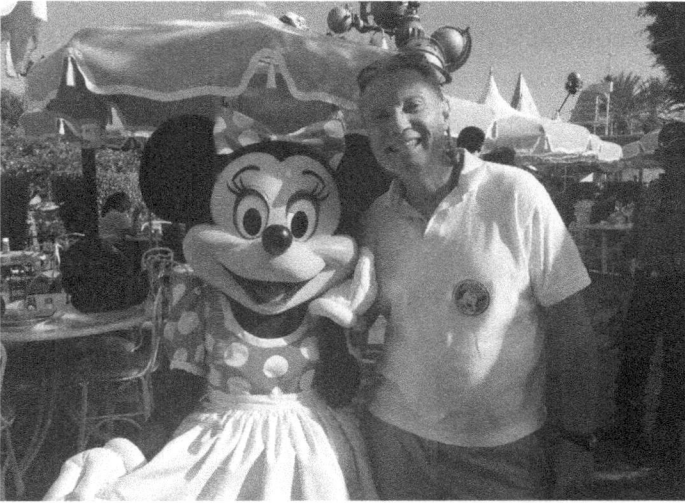

I was having a whole new experience of Disneyland.

A new experience of loving a man.

My man.

My *Freedom*.

We spent a lot of time on the LA freeway. He wanted to show me everything.

He especially wanted to go to The Encinitas Temple. His family wasn't as excited about it as he was because they didn't share the same longing for spiritual questing as Laurence. However, they loved him and agreed to venture there with us.

The temple was founded in 1920 by Paramahansa Yogananda to teach Kriya Yoga, an ancient sacred spiritual science from India. The facility offers lectures, services, scriptural readings, and meditation services. The Ashram and Meditation Gardens have become a center of pilgrimage for thousands of people from all parts of the world. We walked around the temple alongside the ocean. It was quiet, peaceful, and beautiful.

The next day, I asked him if we could go to Hollywood. In Laurence fashion, eager to please, he made it happen. I had forgotten about being there on the trip with my brother as a kid. That's how out of my body I was after my father died. When I saw the concrete display of movie stars on the sidewalk, I immediately recalled my childhood trip.

Hollywood was busy and crowded. We stayed only long enough to go to the Wax Museum and the Dolby Theatre. That was enough for me. Then we took a ride up Rodeo Drive and went window shopping on Sunset Blvd. Fancy stuff!

Gold Lake

The Gold Lake Mountain Resort property we were considering as a place to house our codependency healing center includes one of the largest natural lakes in Boulder County. On the grounds, you can also find ancient Native American ruins. There's a sense of sacredness that makes it a very magical place. The cabins, outdoor hot tubs, meeting rooms and dining hall would all be perfect for our vison of a retreat center.

Laurence and I had nowhere near eleven and a half million dollars needed for the purchase, but we weren't going to let that stop us! We set up an appointment and went to look at the property.

After walking around and seeing the facilities, the realtors told us we could stay as long as we wanted that afternoon. We sat beside the lake with our friend Larry and talked for hours about the healing work we could do there. It felt like home.

Laurence and I got very busy and immediately formed an advisory council of friends who might help us fundraise. Since Joan and Gordon had personally introduced us to David, one of the owners, we were given the opportunity to spend a weekend on the property as potential buyers.

We invited our advisory council up for an experiential weekend of envisioning our healing center. On Halloween weekend, twelve of our friends, known as our *advisory council* shared in the sacredness of the land and the vision.

The winds blew, as they often do at Gold Lake. We honored our ancestors as the Celtic Feast Day, known as Samhain, also fell on October 31st. Samhain is a time when the veil between the worlds is said to be very thin. Therefore, communicating with ancestors can be easier than other times during the year. We invited our friends to bring a relic or photo of an ancestor they wished to acknowledge.

Some of our friends stayed the night in the cabins, and others journeyed home.

Afterwards, several people shared experiences from the day. Here is what my good friend Billie wrote:

I've attached a photo that I took as Patti and I walked around the lake, all the while feeling the wind whip through my hair and the intense cold against my cheeks. And now as I look at the image again, it starts to look more and more like a very large smoke signal...which makes me think of how we were called to come together for a higher purpose. The "announcement" is going out to all and will be visible for miles and miles that this is the sacred gathering place; this is where warring tribes have solved their differences; this is the land of the wounded healers.

Another piece was written by Laurence's cousin, Michelle—

As I made my way out of the foothills and switch-backed down into Boulder, I saw the lights below and felt a sense of trust in myself, my experience and all these new developments. Then in front of me was a street sign, and I couldn't quite figure it out. I focused in on it; it was a unicorn. No, it was Pegasus. No, it was a deer crossing sign; it had antlers. But this deer, focused in, not changing form, had wings and was glowing. It was a deer with wings. And what I got out of it, was, Watch for Angels.

Later in November we had breakfast with David. He told us the property had been leased to a man planning to operate it as an event center. Laurence was very sad. We kept talking about the idea, but the reality of our day-to-day lives kicked in, and the healing center was put on the back burner.

The Love of a Good Woman

Our first kiss began a conversation about whether or not it was time for us to be sexual, or if we should wait. Months later Laurence shared his experience of growing up with his mother and sister in a strict Catholic family. Laurence had tremendous respect for both of them.

His father was mostly unavailable, spending time in bars and coming home drunk.

The Catholic Church had taught Laurence that premarital sex was bad.

He wanted to know how I became comfortable with my sexuality, since I had also been raised Catholic, and had grown up with my devoted mother, my grandmother, and my sister.

I guess the main difference between Laurence and me was that I had been single for eighteen years prior and had asked those same questions long ago.

By this time in my life, I have completely resolved my feelings about sexuality, and come to respect it as an important and healthy aspect of intimate relationship.

For so long sex has been thought of as evil, especially for women.

I could see how Laurence's confusion created shame and guilt about his natural desires.

As a way for me to help Laurence understand my feelings about sex, I shared with him this quote about sex and death from *Shadows of the Sacred* by transpersonal counselor and author Francis Vaughan:

Although death is inevitable, many of us live in denial and avoidance of death, clinging to its unexamined illusions of immortality. These attitudes toward death are reminiscent of Victorian attitudes toward sex that denied the universality of sexual desire. It seems strange that while individual and species survival are the most basic and compelling instincts, the denial of death and the repression of sex are still with us. (p. 49)

One day during our time together, Laurence and I had a healing session with Pedro and Gary, Shamans from Taos. Laurence asked for healing around his sexuality. Pedro's response was, "All you need is the love of a good woman."

Laurence never had any concerns after that. He would often lovingly look at me and say: *"The love of a good woman."*

Laurence loved to write me poetry. Here's one of them that speaks of our intimacy:

Luminescent Light

I want to lose myself gazing into your blue eyes
To hear your beating heart next to mine
To touch and caress each curve and follow every line upon your body
I want to hold you close, collapsing the space between us
Transcending time into a single moment with the whisper of each breath
Letting go, allowing the sandy shore to wash away with waves of love
I want to wrap you in my arms and hold you tight
For you are the rising sun of a new day and the luminescent light of endless,
boundless and timeless sweet new love that has come into the night.
I love you.

I Wanted to Buy You a Ring

On the one-year anniversary of our first date, we went back to Treppedas. I dressed up in a black dress and high heels. We talked about the past year and all our adventures.

We held hands. We were always holding hands.

When we returned home, he handed me a gift bag. Inside was a ring box. I wasn't sure what to think. We had talked about getting married, possibly in France. But that night, he just handed me the bag.

I opened the box inside the bag and saw a gold wedding band.

"What am I supposed to do with this? This is a wedding ring."

"I just knew I wanted to get you a ring. I planned to ask you to marry me in France, but I couldn't wait."

"So, are you asking me to marry you?"

"Yes, will you marry me?"

"Yes?"

It's a good thing Laurence didn't mind that I had an occasional glass of wine. That night I'd had two at dinner. I was a bit upset at the proposal. For several reasons. One, it was a wedding ring and not an engagement ring. Two, I had to ask him if he was asking me to marry him before he actually did. Three, I remembered the last reading he'd had with our friend Elisa, the medium. Suzan came through, and asked Laurence what he was waiting for. Laurence had interpreted that to mean he should marry me now, and not wait.

His memories of Suzan and his occasional meetings with Elisa were becoming a sore spot for me. One night I had a dream that he and Suzan were still married, and I was his mistress. That was how I felt sometimes. I shared the dream with him, and he apologized. But the bottom line was he wasn't over her. And I could never replace her.

A month before he'd moved in, he still had his wedding picture on his nightstand. When I mentioned that it bothered me, he said he was planning to pack it away when he moved. He didn't think it was a problem. I asked him how he would feel if I had a picture of Ken on my nightstand. He then got it. He put the wedding picture in a drawer after that.

But the ghost was still in the room.

Even though I *said* yes, I was having doubts. Was I only there to numb his pain? Was it a matter of time before he realized that, and our perfect romance would come crashing down?

I concluded there was time to find out. We weren't married. Just engaged.

And I loved him.

A lot.

I explained the difference between engagement and wedding rings to him.

He told me he would take the ring back and get me what I wanted.

He eventually revealed that he had bought the ring at Costco, thinking a jeweler would have unfairly higher prices on wedding rings.

Coincidentally, later that night we saw a segment on the news about Costco selling less than authentic diamond rings!

We lay in bed watching it together and laughed.

We were engaged.

Will You Marry Me?

For Thanksgiving, we drove to Tucson, Arizona to pick up my mom's large antique secretary from my sister's new house. On the way we stopped in Santa Fe. I told him it would be fun to look at rings there.

As soon as we arrived, we parked and walked to the plaza. Looking at the price tags on the engagement rings, I could almost hear his inner gasp. I didn't want him to spend too much. I was searching for something reasonable.

In one jewelry store I described what I wanted: something colorful and curvy. He walked down the counter and said, "How about this one?"

The ring was set in yellow gold with tanzanite, diamonds, and opals. I slipped it on my ring finger. It fit perfectly. The price was a little less than some we had seen, but it wasn't cheap. I worried about money and how much we were spending.

He looked at me and said, "I really want to buy you this ring. Let me know if it's the one you want." I looked at the ring. I looked at Laurence. I felt how perfectly it fit on my finger.

"Yes."

He paid for the ring and then told me to take it off. He put it back into the box. He asked the jeweler how to get to the closest Mexican restaurant. We walked there and ordered dinner. Chiles rellenos for Laurence, of course.

He took my hand, gazed into my eyes and said, "I love you. You are my best friend. I want to spend the rest of my life with you. Will you marry me?"

No hesitation from me this time.

"Yes!"

We drove to Tucson the next day and had Thanksgiving with my sister, brother-in-law, and their friends. Laurence and Paul took off the following day on motorcycles. Mary and I went for a hike at Saguaro National Park.

We all met up for dinner at a restaurant Laurence liked. It had the best chiles rellenos anywhere, or so he said.

The following day we headed back to Denver. In Santa Fe, we met up again with Joan and Gordon for breakfast. Laurence told them the news, and on the way out of the restaurant, Joan bought us a pot holder as an engagement gift.

We called our families in the car on the way home.

It was official.

We were getting married.

The question everyone asked, of course, was "When?"

We had no idea.

Being engaged was perfect for now.

I'm Not Suzan

We had traveled so much all year that we decided to stay home for our first Christmas living together. I thought it would be nice to cook a turkey, just the two of us. We planned the menu and the day. For the most part, we always did well together, negotiating what and how we wanted to do things.

As the turkey and other side dishes were cooking, Laurence was peeling potatoes in the sink. I told him my garbage disposal didn't work very well, and it might be better to dispose of the peels in the trash can. He didn't take my advice. The garbage disposal stopped up. As dinner was cooking, he got out his tools and crawled under the sink.

I couldn't get around him to finish preparing the meal. He was grumbling about my dishwasher while telling me the one that he and Suzan had was so much better than *mine*.

There she was again: Suzan.

He fixed the disposal. We had dinner.

But something just didn't feel right.

Stage One

In the New Year, my relationship fears got triggered. He often prefaced what we were doing with "Suzan and I always..." or, "Suzan said..." I didn't mind being patient with his grief process, but I was *not* so patient with him comparing me to her.

I also worried about his poor time and money management. Being late to our first date didn't bother me at the time. I later learned, however, that he was *frequently* tardy.

And he was *horrible* at managing money. One day he randomly said out loud, "I have no idea how much money I spend." Honestly, that freaked me out a bit.

I had developed a way to manage time and money that was *very* different from his. He thought I worried too much about it. I thought he didn't worry enough.

I suggested we start weekly meetings to discuss our schedules and our budget. Talking openly about it, we could negotiate both areas.

Money was never important to me. I don't care about status, cars, or material goods. But I do have to work hard to keep a roof over my head and meet my basic needs. I almost lost my house to foreclosure the year before and I'd borrowed money to keep it.

Laurence took over many of the expenses, which helped tremendously. But when I discovered how he managed money I worried, as we were both newly self-employed and drowning in the same ship.

He said he wanted to take care of me and support me as I continued to develop my career. I trusted him completely, but the numbers terrified me. No retirement. No solid financial plans. I could manage my own anxiety about money, but I wasn't sure how to manage it in partnership. I had been doing it all alone for so long.

I didn't know how to explain what I was feeling without hurting him. I knew he was a man of his word and that I could trust him, but my somatic response was terror. How would we survive?

I began holing up in my little home office, not knowing how to talk about my fears. Even though we always talked about everything, this one was hard. My introspection triggered Laurence's abandonment fears, and a behavior he had mentioned previously, one he had hoped I'd never see, reared its ugly head. Rage.

He started yelling about my distance. I wasn't sure how to respond to some of the things he was saying. To me, he seemed a bit irrational. I let him rage, all the while wondering what was happening. Was this going to be a repeat of my marriage? My ex-husband had been verbally, emotionally, and physically abusive. I wasn't at all interested in *that* again. It was alarming.

Once he'd calmed down, we talked through what had happened. He said he wanted to learn how not to react to me that way, because he realized I had trauma from my first marriage. He believed that it was necessary for couples to fight in order to resolve conflict. My concern was that he wasn't going to be able to fight without raging.

In the hope of better managing his anger, he registered for *The Hoffman Process* in California. Hoffman offers week-long healing retreats for people who are feeling stuck in one or more areas of their life. We found the Hoffman Program while working on our vision of a healing center for codependency. Hoffman seemed aligned with our goals for healing personally and professionally. It was perfect timing for him to attend, as we had hit what I called *a wall* of misunderstanding in our relationship.

While he was gone, I experienced post-traumatic stress disorder symptoms as a result of his temper, triggering memories of my ex-husband's abuse. I couldn't sleep. I worried about whether or not I had made the wrong decision by having him move in. I was scared I might be repeating the past. It all felt so foreign to the Laurence I had known.

When he returned home a week later, I posed the question about whether or not we moved in together too quickly. He took that as a rejection and immediately went to his computer to find a new place to live. I was willing to work on the relationship, but he made an abrupt decision to leave.

It was a very emotional time for both of us. *Stage one* of my grief began, as if I had a terminal illness. The beginning of the end seemed near. I wanted to fight the relationship cancer but wasn't sure how we would survive. It was hard.

One month later he moved out. That morning we sat on the sofa together with our coffee as we normally did in our daybreak routine. Holding hands, he said, "I don't think many people would be doing this as well as we are!"

I agreed.

He rented a house close to where he lived as a child in Denver. He thought living there would give him a chance to heal more of his childhood wounds from his father's alcoholism and abandonment. He was determined to face his fears of being alone.

Even though he moved out March 1st, we were still deeply in love.

We both intuitively knew living apart was the right thing to do. I again proposed the *ninety days, no contact* idea, thinking it would give him time to be alone. He agreed. We said goodbye. He moved out. I put my furniture back in place, rehung my paintings, and then called him the next day. I missed my best friend. I didn't know how not to talk to him. We both decided ninety days apart was a bad idea.

We found a couples counselor and began long-distance dating again.

The drive down to see him was difficult for me. I wasn't sleeping well and had to work long hours to build my private practice. Without his financial household contributions, I once again was living on the brink of foreclosure.

Laurence continued to be his kind, sweet self. He came to my house more than I went to Denver. He offered to continue to help me with projects and yard work. We played a lot of Scrabble.

We had an ongoing Scrabble competition, and he kept a record of our final scores on his phone. He was so proud to always be able to say his high score was 384 and that the closest I ever came to that was 341. However, the words that were *not* spoken were the ones about how we would ever resolve the geographical dilemma. I had no idea how we could ever get back to *us*.

Marva and Ed

The week that Laurence moved out was also the week my next-door neighbor and dear friend Marva was in the hospital awaiting a second open-heart surgery. Her valve replacement surgery in October had left her with shortness of breath and extreme fatigue. She never recovered. After subsequent lung surgeries, other treatments, and finally a second open-heart surgery, she passed away on March 15, 2016.

I spent many nights on the phone with Laurence crying and grieving, both his moving out, and Marva's dying. He listened patiently for long periods of time and was more than willing to hold the space for my grief. I wailed; he listened. It felt bittersweet to know he was listening and there for me, but at the same time, no longer living with me. It was a double-edged sword.

Shortly after Marva's death, her beloved partner Ed moved to Tucson, Arizona. Marva and Ed had been like parents to me. Whenever something broke in my house, Ed fixed it. When Marva was shopping, she remembered what I liked and bought me little gifts. When cleaning out her cabinets and closets, she frequently brought over items saying, "Would you have any use for this?" With the big signature smile on her face that everyone loved, she was always there when I needed her.

And then one day she was gone.

And then Ed was gone, too.

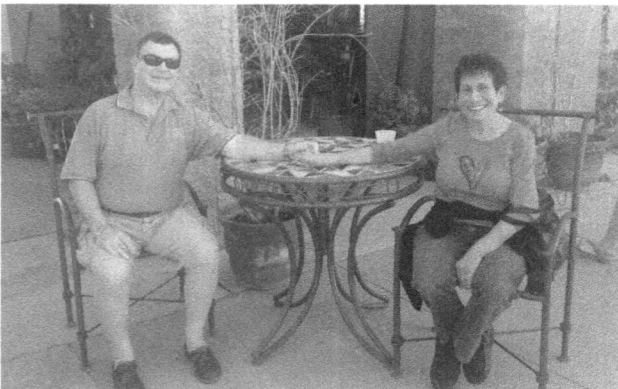

Howling at the Moon

And then, another loss. A few days after Ed left for Arizona, Laurence and I made the decision to put our beloved Jasper to sleep. Jasper had a breathing obstruction that was making it hard for him to take in air.

Laurence and I felt he was too old and fragile for the indicated surgery. The veterinarian concurred that it was kinder to let him go.

Laurence and I didn't fear death. We watched the doctors at University Hospital try to keep Marva alive and both agreed we didn't wish to have our lives prolonged that way. It was painful to witness Marva's suffering, knowing that it wasn't likely that she would ever have any quality of life again. Laurence and I discussed getting a living will and a DNR (Do Not Resuscitate) order created to ensure that we would not have to go through the pain of living connected to wires and tubes for too long.

We knew Jasper was in tremendous pain and ready to go. Even though it was hard to let him go, we both knew it was time.

The morning after we left the veterinarian's office, Laurence and I had breakfast at a local café and sat outside on the patio. In my mind, I imagined Jasper in the sky, howling with a sense of joy and freedom. No longer in pain. Happy and grateful that we were able to let him go.

Surrendering to Greater Possibilities

A few days after we put Jasper to sleep, we left for a spiritual journey to Mexico with our newly found friend and spiritual teacher, Lee McCormick. In addition to his treatment center in Nashville, Lee owns a retreat center near Teotihuacan, where he hosts spiritual journeys several times a year.

Teotihuacan is northeast of Mexico City and was built between the first and seventh centuries A.D.. Ruins, monuments, and pyramids, all based on geometric and symbolic principles are what is left of this ancient city.

Prior to leaving for the trip I told Laurence I was worried about the challenges of our geographic differences. He liked living in Denver. I liked living in Niwot. I couldn't think of a way to work that out. I couldn't find a treatment for our terminal illness. We loved being together, yet our new lifestyles created challenges that neither of us knew how to solve.

That morning, he said to me, "The one thing I know for sure is that I love you and I want to be with you. I don't have a solution, but I have a feeling we might get some answers on our trip to Mexico."

I left it at that. Off to Mexico we went; we were good travelers together.

The journey was quite incredible. Hats off to Lee McCormick for holding such a sacred space for everyone on the journey. Each day, we walked to the pyramids from the colorful retreat center. Lee told us the history and then guided us through meditation and ritual. Each night we got together with the group and shared our experiences of the day.

When Laurence and I returned home, I was sick with traveler's diarrhea, or what's often referred to as *Montezuma's Revenge*. Once I was feeling better, Laurence told me about an experience that he'd been afraid to tell me about on the trip.

Part of the week's adventure included a three-hour drive to Tolantongo, MX: a sweet spot off the beaten path that has gorgeous hot

springs, warm cave baths, and waterfalls.

Laurence was an explorer, and sometimes a little deviant. In one of the caves, he swam under a rope marked *do not enter*. He was immediately pulled underwater and struggled to reemerge. He thought he was going to die.

He was afraid to tell me because he didn't want to upset me. Thinking about it now, I wonder; *was that our answer?* There wasn't going to be a cure for our cancer. Maybe almost drowning was preparing us for what was to come, and the answer was: *he was going to die.*

A few weeks after he told me of his near-death experience, he wrote this blog:

Surrendering to Greater Possibilities

I have had two significant surrender experiences in my lifetime. The first one I stood at the cliff of uncertainty drawn to this point of letting go and jumping into the abyss of the unknown from my active addiction and living a double life. I remember this surrender experience as vividly today, even though it has been over thirty-five years since I made that fateful leap of surrender.

My mind was screaming at me to hide, to retreat to find a way out and to not "LET GO!" Another softer part of my mind invited me to jump, to let go, to surrender and allow myself to fall into a cargo net of God's love.

I did not know what my fate would be if I let go, if I surrendered, and confessed about my addiction, my charade of living two lives, I could be publicly humiliated, I could be unemployed and divorced from breaking my code of silence and telling my secret.

On that day, I chose to jump into the unknown, risking these dire life consequences. In return, I was carried from the cargo net of God's love to a new life free from the hold of my addiction and placed upon the road called "the sunshine of the Spirit."

The second surrender experience was only weeks ago. I surrendered to the undercurrent of water that drew me deeper into a dark cave and plunged me further and deeper down into a bottomless pool of water. After three attempts to free myself from the undertow grip, I surrendered, accepting my fate of my life's ending. Once I surrendered, I was spun 360 degrees and jettisoned out to the opposite side of the cavern where I could stand up and walk out. By surrendering to death, accepting my fate of mortality, I was lifted up and I was saved.

As I walked back out to the shore, I could hear voices speaking to me: "You are taken care of. It would also be a lot easier, if you would not work so hard and just let us help you."

Giving up and letting go of control is not easy. It is instinctual to fight, to resist, and to hold on for dear life. Aspects of self-preservation, self-reliance, and self-survival are all parts of being human.

What I have learned is that I am not alone and that I have an army of invisible helpers from the other side standing by me that love me. By surrendering I am guided, I am cared for, I am protected, and I am carried into a greater life of possibilities that far exceed my deepest dreams and desires.

Stage Two

A month after we got back from Mexico, my daughter and her five-year-old son came to visit me for my birthday. My son and his girlfriend also came for two days.

Laurence assumed I would spend the entire Fourth of July weekend with him, while I had only planned on spending two nights with him. He was angry. He thought I was avoiding him again, like when I spent time alone in my office when we lived together. I was not.

I was running a household alone again and struggling to pay bills. I needed to clean my house and get ready for my family to visit. I couldn't spend every second I had in Denver. It was really taking a lot out of me to do this long-distance relationship. I wanted to be with him, but instead of the relationship feeling supportive it now felt like pure exhaustion. Maybe the cancer had spread, and we had advanced to *Stage Two*. Harder to treat.

I told him he'd have to decide if what I could give was enough or not. He said he would think about it. It was an awful phone call. No ladybugs that night.

The next day he apologized and said he understood my burnout. Perhaps it was good for him, he suggested. It gave him more time to learn to be alone and manage his codependency. He told me he loved me and wanted to be with me. He was willing to continue to see how we could work things out.

I was relieved and happy to still be planning my birthday celebration with both him and my family. Laurence wanted to take us all to the Fort, an award-winning restaurant south of Denver famous for its western atmosphere. We drove down on my birthday and stopped at Red Rocks Amphitheatre and then Tiny Town, a miniature replica of a Colorado town. My grandson loved Tiny Town. I loved it all.

Laurence spent a lot of time with us during their visit. He got us tickets to a Rockies game. He and my grandson hit golf balls in his backyard: fun for Laurence because the energetic four-year-old would run and retrieve his golf balls.

Once everyone left, Laurence and I continued to fight our relationship cancer.

Stage Three

I stayed exhausted. Laurence continued to come up to my house more often than I went to Denver. We played a lot of Scrabble, but never found the right words to fix us. *Still.*

I was going back to my old modus operandi of wanting to get rid of the good guy. *I didn't need him anyway; I had been single for a long time; I was better alone.* Those were the thoughts that frequented my mind. I had no cure for this terminal illness. Were we now in *Stage Three*?

I was less patient with his quirky behaviors concerning time management and forgetfulness, angry when he wouldn't wear his hearing aid, angry that I no longer felt heard by him. He was the one person who *really* heard me! Why did he seem so far away now?

I started to wonder if we were ever going to be able to work out our differences. My fear of being in a relationship was coming back, and I was beginning to avoid and run from him. I was less available for calls and getting together, and I was short with him on the phone.

As a result, Laurence and I began to wonder if we were really *a match*. Even though I knew we had challenges, and I wasn't being the best partner I could be, I was still angry and confused. He had promised to never leave me. We had many good things together. When I asked Laurence if he wanted to work things out, he replied with this text:

I have been contemplating your question on whether I think we can work things out. This is what I know, I love you, because of that, I would like to work things out, but I have two concerns. 1) The uncertainty if our differences are so different that we are not able to work them out. 2) Knowing my tendency to adapt and being quick to say yes, let's work this out to stop how much pain I'm in, which potentially risks betraying both of us.... I have a proposal, to put us on hold for ninety days. Instinctively I have known that I need to go through the be-alone experience without the security of a relationship. I believe the time apart will provide you time to heal and for both of us to determine whether we believe we can work out our differences for a long-term relationship. What do you think?

My reply was *yes, that's a great idea*. And then the *REAL* ninety days began. I truly wanted him to be sure he wanted to be with me because it was the right thing for both of us, not because he was afraid to be alone. The idea that I'd suggested early in our relationship might be our cure. Maybe ninety days apart was a *codependency chemotherapy*: we had to kill both the good and bad cells to get rid of the cancer.

It was hard to be without him. I really missed our calls, texts, and weekend adventures. However, I knew if we could get through this time, we would be stronger and better together.

We made an agreement that we wouldn't contact each other for ninety days. If there was an emergency, or something work-related, we'd be in touch. Other than that, we would have *no* contact. Both of us honored the commitment and kept to the agreement, *fairly well*.

I did text a few times in my grief and despair. One particular night, I was really hurting. The grief was intense. I wailed like my mother had when my father died. I loved him *that* much.

He offered that we could get together, because he wanted to be sure I was okay. He was willing to see me because of how much pain I was in. At least his codependency said that. It might have been that he, too, wanted to numb out his pain.

At first, I said yes, and we planned to watch the Broncos together on Sunday.

After more reflection, I decided it was a bad idea. I knew Laurence well enough to know that if we saw each other that day, he would want to enter back into the ninety-day agreement after we said goodbye. I didn't want to restart my grieving all over again. I thought it best to stay the course and live out the full three months as originally planned.

The Cure

The last month of our separation we were a little more conversational.

In October he went back to Kauai to honor what would have been the nineteenth wedding anniversary for him and Suzan.

While he was away, I was busy preparing for a weekend retreat.

It was the first time I had held a retreat since 2012. I have been offering experiential weekend retreats for mothers since 2005, based on the findings in my doctoral dissertation about women not feeling good enough. In these retreats, I facilitate art, music, dance, ritual, poetry, and other activities for the purpose of embodying the material, and not just intellectualizing it.

The retreat that year was happening on the same weekend that Laurence and I had brought the group to Gold Lake the year before. So again, in light of it being Samhain, we spent some time honoring our ancestors in the sacred circle.

Prior to the weekend beginning, I received an e-mail from Laurence letting me know that Pedro, the Mexican-American Healer we knew, had died suddenly a few days before. It was quite a shock to hear the news of Pedro's death. He died of an enlarged heart.

"The love of a good woman" was the response I put in my e-mail back to him regarding Pedro's passing. Laurence's response was: "You are a good woman."

I was having very unsettling feelings that weekend that I couldn't quite understand. I wasn't nervous about the retreat because I had held many of them prior to that one. I wasn't really upset that Laurence was in Hawaii without me, because I knew this was an important thing for him to do. I couldn't quite figure out what it was.

Here are a few of our e-mail messages from that day:

Oct 28 @ 1:33 pm

Hi Patti;

I am sending lots of love, light and blessings upon you and your workshop participants this weekend. I have continued to keep you in the forefront of my mind knowing this is the weekend for you to share your gifts and wisdom with the women in your workshop. I have no doubt it will be a great success. I miss you too, and I can't help but think back on the magic and wonderful time we shared when we were both out here. Truly very lovely memories, it would be nice to be creating more, with you being here this time as well, but obviously this was not meant to be. You have also shown up in two of my dreams since coming out here, so for whatever it's worth my subconscious has you here.

On Nov. 1st. I will be traveling out to the North Shore and spending time at the place where Suzan and I spoke our wedding vows, nineteen years ago. Coming back and visiting this place on what would have been our nineteen-year wedding anniversary is what I am being called to do. I am not sure of the why, I am just trusting the intuitive knowing and seeing what transpires and revealed in doing so.

I miss seeing, talking, hanging, making love, as well as beating you at Scrabble and Backgammon, as well as our projects together!

Have a great, awesome workshop, shine your light bright.

Love, Laurence

Oct 28 @ 1:52 pm

Hi Laurence:

Curious about the dreams.???

It will be nice to see you again. I am remembering this time last year we were planning for Gold Lake.

I feel like something is missing not having you here with me. I am trying to hold back and not say anything, but today I feel so very alone without you.

I have such an unsettledness about this day?? I hope the retreat goes well and yet something feels weird. I guess I am processing it already?

Miss telling you about my life.

Love,

Patti

Oct 28 2:34 pm

Patti;

I am with you in spirit, and as noted; I have been sending lots of blessings your way as well as offering up prayers for your workshop. I know your workshop will be inspiring, and powerful for all who attend. I too am looking forward to getting to see and catch up with you as well.

Shine baby, shine, L

Then he e-mailed me a picture from our trip to Mexico. With the short message: *"Our adventure."* It was good to be connecting again. I was hoping our *codependency cancer* was close to cured. Maybe when we got back together after the ninety days, we would be cancer-free.

I Am So Grateful for This Moment

I was very angry at the beginning of the ninety days. The anger helped create distance between us. But after a while, I was just mostly sad.

He was my best friend. He was my companion. My soulmate, if you will. He was worth waiting ninety days for. I was willing to do whatever it might take for us to have a healthy relationship. Yet, I deeply feared never being with him again.

Ten weeks into the ninety days, I went to see Brené Brown speak at Mile Hi Church. I felt a strong intuition to share her talk, *Rising Strong as a Spiritual Practice*, with Laurence. I texted him to see if he might be willing to have dinner with me since the lecture was so close to his house. I thought the lecture might set the stage for the conversations I wanted to have with him about repairing our relationship. I'd been thinking a lot about my part in our break-up. I wanted so much to be back with him again. I couldn't stop thinking about what went wrong and how we could fix it. Only a few more weeks to go.

He quickly said yes. We spent the afternoon and evening together.

I apologized for my self-righteousness, judgment, and impatience that had colored part of our time together, prior to the ninety-day separation decision.

We sat for a long time on the sofa as he held me in his arms. Touching his skin felt like Heaven. It was so good to see him again. I sighed and said, "I am so grateful for this moment."

Similar to the night we first made love, we weren't sure if it was the right thing to do, but we did it anyway. We made love. It's one decision I will never regret.

I was happy to be close to the end of this long separation.

As we lay next to each other, skin to skin, he randomly said:

"I think it's harder to lose a partner through death than divorce."

"*I* don't think so," I responded.

Then I explained *why* I believed divorce was harder.

I shared a story about shopping with my widowed mother as a

teenager and meeting a woman who was divorced. My mother told the woman that she believed it was harder to be divorced than widowed, because after a marriage ends you still have to see the person who left. My mom explained that even though losing her husband was devastating, she knew it was final and she was forced to move on with her life.

I also told Laurence how difficult it was for me after Ken and I broke up. I grieved for years and longed to be with him. If Ken had died, I would have had no other choice than to move on, which may have been easier to accept. I *thought*.

One of my favorite movies is *Under the Tuscan Sun*. In the movie Diane Lane plays a recently divorced woman who moves to Italy and impulsively buys a villa. One day, when she was struggling to make it work in her new home, her realtor came to help her find a snake.

She said to him: "Do you know what the most surprising thing about divorce is? It doesn't actually kill you, like a bullet to the heart or a head-on car wreck. It should. When someone you've promised to cherish until death do you part says he never loved you, it should kill you instantly. You shouldn't have to wake up day after day after something like that, trying to understand how in the world you didn't know" (Sternberg & Wells, 2003).

After my divorce, and other serious relationship endings, I felt like I should have died because the pain was so bad. I would sometimes wish and hope about reconciling, while idealizing the relationship after it ended. I wanted to have what I *imagined* it could be, rather than what it *was*. OVER!

That last night Laurence and I were together, he told me he was feeling a lot of fear. He didn't want to hurt me. Laurence was fearless: a daredevil and an adrenal junkie; this big fear was a side of Laurence I hadn't seen before. I told him he had already hurt me, and that fear was part of being in relationship. We have to take the risk of being hurt in order to fully love.

We agreed to try to work things out, but he wanted to completely finish the ninety days to be clear on how to be in a relationship again. I agreed. It was only two more weeks. I loved him so much, I was willing to go the distance.

I'll Be Better When You Call Me Darling

Laurence and I talked on the phone for over two hours the night of the presidential election, November 8, 2016. I was worried about the future of our country with Donald Trump as president. I told Laurence I needed him more than ever during these trying times.

The next day he sent me a text to see how I was. I told him I was happy to hear from him and would be even better if he called me *darling*. He called immediately, but the ringer on my phone was turned off.

Hey Darling. I just picked up your response, and you said it would help you smile if I gave you a call. So, I was just following up and giving you a call. No need to call me back. I'm pretty pooped out. Got to bed late and didn't sleep really well, so I'm moving in the direction of going to bed early, but I hope you get a good night's sleep tonight. I guess we'll talk soon. All right, I love you. Bye, bye.

Then, the next morning he sent this text:

Good Morning. I am going to step back into our original agreement and finish out the ninety days, no contact. In the interim please know- I do love you and I am praying/meditating and thinking about our conversation and looking for middle ground to be in a relationship and also be in integrity with myself, and you. Let me know what time you want me to come on Saturday the 19th and I will be there. Much love coming to you.

In my text back to him, I told him I was writing him love letters and that I'd already mailed two of them. I asked if he wanted me to hold onto the rest of them, like I did when he was in Brazil. He suggested I hang onto them, so he could keep his head clear.

The next day Leonard Cohen passed away. Laurence loved Cohen's music. Naturally, I wanted to reach out to him when I heard the news. But I honored his request to not have any more contact until our date on November 19th. I didn't call. I didn't text.

Instead I went shopping for a sexy outfit for our date and continued to write him love letters that I was saving for him in a hand-painted box.

Love Letters to Freedom

I wrote Laurence seven letters in that last week before he died. Letters one and two were hand-written. The first one I sent on Election Day, prior to knowing the results before we talked on the phone that night.

Later that same day I wrote letter number two on an article I printed from the internet about a Hans Christian Anderson fairy tale, *The Princess and the Pea*. I had had a dream the night before that made me think of the story, and I thought it might be relevant to our healing.

Letter #2

My Love,

Last night I had a dream that I titled, "Sweet Pea."

We were at a Jungian lecture and there was new leadership and a lot of disorganization. I was sitting between you (on my right) and a large unknown man (on my left). I felt crowded and uncomfortable. I left to get out of the crowd. I was walking around outside the big conference room in a quieter room. You found me during the break, looking confused and nervous. You said they had been talking about a "Sweet Pea" story. You asked if I knew about it and understood it, because you didn't understand what they were saying. I said I didn't know, but I could look it up online. I started searching to see what I could find. (end of dream)

I woke up at 4:00 am this morning and couldn't get back to sleep. I decided to write and mail you letters this week to show you how much I love you and want to be with you. I mailed letter number one today, and I will mail this letter number two tomorrow.

The dream reminded me of the fairy tale, The Princess and the Pea. I'm sending you this version of the story, with a Jungian analysis by Kay Nielsen. I don't know how it might be relevant to us, but it struck me as important to share. xxxooo, Patti

---

I sent him the fairy tale and the interpretation by Kay Nielsen. She says the story is about "the soul's longing for itself." It asks the question: "Who do I belong with and how will I know them?...The Prince, our questing, achieving self is lonely. It is always lonely, always set apart. Its quest is two-fold: to find the princess who will cure his loneliness; and to recognize her."

Letter # 3, I wrote the day after the election:

Letter #3

November 9, 2016

Dearest Laurence:

Today we have a new president, and a new world for sure. It's hard to believe and is so very scary to be without you as it is happening. I am glad we talked last night. I have so much to say to you and want so much to share my heart with you. The days we have been apart have taught me so much about my fear and my love for you.

Remember when you were in Brazil and I wrote you a letter a day? I have so much love inside for you that I again decided to write you a letter a day as I await our "date."

Good night my love. I was so happy to hear your voice on the phone saying "Darling" and "I love you."

My Darling, I love you, too.

Writing letters helped me express all the emotion I was feeling. I anxiously awaited our date. I had a deep fear I may never see him again. It didn't make sense. Laurence had always adored me, and I adored him. Why was I so worried? I wonder now if that is all part of the mystery. Some things we think we *know*, but we can't *ever* really *know*!

PART THREE
Grace

"The enchanted issue is not whether bodies stay together or not; but whether hearts and minds are reconciled."

MARIANNE WILLIAMSON, *Enchanted Love*

The Phone Call

The night before I learned that Laurence had died, I finished painting the box for his letters. My friend Billie was sleeping over after a long night of doing art together. We built a fire in the backyard and sat under the huge, bright November super moon. I felt a calm presence as if Laurence was there with me in my heart. I hoped he would still choose to be with me, but somehow, I felt he was gone.

The next morning, we watched a clip from *Saturday Night Live*. Kate McKinnon, in character as Hillary Clinton, sang *Hallelujah* in honor of Leonard Cohen's passing and Hillary's lost election. After watching the video, Billie and I continued to sing the song *Hallelujah* for a long while. We commented on how we just couldn't get the song out of our heads.

Billie left. I turned on the Broncos game and finished letter # 7.

Two hours later I got the call from Laurence's friend Jim, telling me he had just found Laurence dead on his living room floor.

The Empty Shoes

I jumped into my car and started driving to Denver. When I arrived at Laurence's house, Junia, Jim, and another friend were sitting on the front porch. The police officer had taken the body and locked the door, since no one there was a family member.

I had the key. I opened the door. We entered, stunned and silent.

Two other friends arrived later. We sat in a circle around the spot where Laurence's body had been found. I looked to my right and saw his empty canvas shoes. I placed them in the center of us. All eyes on the shoes, we cried, and we prayed, we prayed, and we cried. We cried again and prayed some more.

What else was there to do? Oh yes: we shared stories. And we laughed about some of the funny memories we'd each had with Laurence. He would have wanted us to laugh.

What's *next*? His clients? His things? His family? What?

His brother flew in the next day. His sister would arrive later in the week along with other relatives. His brother was going to tell Laurence's thirty-five-year-old son that his father had died.

Listening

Junia offered to stay as long as I needed after everyone else had left.

I reached for Laurence's box of *Angel Cards* on the end table.

When Laurence and I were together, we typically started our day with meditation and prayer. Doreen Virtue's inspirational cards were often part of that practice. I picked up the box, pulled the card titled *Listening*. The card spoke to listening to inner guidance and letting go of any doubts about whether or not you are really communicating with your angels.

Then, I closed my eyes and listened.

What I heard may have been my imagination; or perhaps Laurence?

I can take better care of you from here. You are going to be okay. You are never alone.

That night I slept alone in his bed. I can still clearly see and feel his midnight blue sheets. His smell embraced my aching heart. I surely did feel alone, and I had *no* idea how I would *ever* be okay again. It was hard to breathe. It was even harder to stay alive.

Are You Okay?

The words, *you are going to be okay,* reminded me of an e-mail I had gotten from Laurence during our ninety-day separation. It read:

> This lady bug showed up and landed upon my leg for a visit, so I had to take a picture, and share it with you. I hope you are doing okay.

I responded: *Okay isn't congruent with grief. I am barely holding on.*

I remember the feeling I had in my chest that one night during our separation. I thought I was having a heart attack. I couldn't breathe. I cried and wailed and my whole body ached. I texted Laurence late that night and told him it felt like he was dead, even though he wasn't. He reassured me that he wasn't going anywhere and reminded me how much he loved me.

Still, I feared he was gone forever.

I grieved.

I ached from the back of my heart.

You Are Never Alone

When I was thirty-three I attended a workshop with renowned counselor and teacher, John Bradshaw. He led us in a guided meditation where we met a guide. I saw my father sitting across from me and saying, *"You are never, ever alone."*

I think of those words often. According to some spiritual texts I've read, separation is an illusion. We're all part of a Oneness, or Essence, and what many call God. Therefore, we are never alone.

But knowing that we're never alone, doesn't take away the grief we must feel as humans. Every day I long for the touch, the smell, the taste, the kiss, and the comfort of the togetherness we had created. The depth of my love is measured by the depth of my pain. I would give anything to hear Laurence say, *Hi Darling*, once more. The heartache of never being with him again, coexists with the truth that I am never, ever alone.

My grief is a passage into deeper aspects of myself, somewhat like a magical mystery ride. I am honoring the process, and at the same time, I do feel Laurence is always with me. I know I am never alone, and paradoxically, I will grieve as long as I must for lack of his physical presence.

Hallelujah

I was grateful to have been able to participate in the planning of Laurence's service. After he died, I felt a bit awkward since we had been taking a break in our relationship. I told Dr. Patty that I had no idea who I was to him anymore, but I was going to go with *girlfriend,* since we had a date scheduled for the following week to begin our relationship anew.

When planning the memorial service, some of Laurence's friends requested that the song *Hallelujah* be played. My friend Billie, who had been singing it with me the morning he died didn't know we had planned to have it sung during the service.

After the memorial she told me how profound and moving it was to hear it played that day for Laurence. She burst into tears and grabbed our friend Donna's arm when she heard it. She couldn't help but wonder if it was Laurence that we felt that morning when we couldn't stop singing *Hallelujah.*

Laurence's son and I concurred that the song "If I Die Before You," written by Laurence's friend Cheryl Wheeler would be played at the recessional. It is a funny song about what is left for the other after someone dies. Laurence loved to laugh, and he loved Cheryl.

Much different from my father's funeral, I actually chuckled a bit while walking out of the sanctuary! I had a feeling that Laurence was laughing, too! He had a strange sense of humor. Here are a few lines the song:

> *If I die before you*
> *it might not be all bad.*
> *You can turn down the heat.*
> *You can turn up the ads.*
> *You can reset the toaster*
> *to maximum roast*
> *and then butter the cinders*
> *you like to call toast.*

I will send you a message
if ever I can,
just to tell you I'm fine
and it's not quite the end.
Or I might not be able,
I might just be dead,
or it might really be
as hot as they said.

All Depression is Unresolved Grief

After Laurence died, everything I knew about grief from having lost my father and subsequently becoming a therapist was tucked away somewhere in my mind. However, grief exists in the heart, not the head. So, it didn't matter what I knew. It just hurt like hell. Every part of my body, mind and heart *hurt*. His sudden death sent me into what felt like a time warp, or a walk-through molasses. No words can quite describe it.

The one thing I did know was that I needed to allow the feelings to surface in order to get through the pain. I remember my first day of graduate school in 1989. The professor, who was also a therapist, wrote these words on the board:

All depression is unresolved grief.

That hit me like a ton of bricks.

When I was eleven, I didn't realize that adults might not be giving me the best advice, such as *I should be happy that Daddy was in Heaven.* Instead I concluded there must be something wrong with me. Depression laid heavily on top of my shame about feeling sad when I was a child.

As a result of that graduate class I found a therapist. I worked slowly and steadily through my unresolved grief. I wailed and screamed in the shower. I wrote my father letters. I felt deep sadness that I thought was going to kill me, and at times it *did* drown me in my dreams. Large waves coming at me from all directions, with no sight of shore had become a common nightmare during my grief process.

Another recurring dream I frequently had after my father died was me running out the front door of my parent's house to get away from an intruder. I would try to find shelter in a neighbor's house, so I wouldn't be captured and killed. In waking life, the front entrance of my parent's house was the place where I had seen my father's corpse the day he died.

After a year of working through my unresolved grief that dream stopped.

Maybe the dream was telling me the same thing my college professor had written on the chalkboard: *All depression is unresolved grief.*

When Laurence died, I made a commitment to myself to give sorrow words and grieve fully. I paid close attention to what came up, and I honored my feelings.

Psychologist Carl Jung said, "What we resist persists and oftentimes grows larger."

I allow my grief to be what it is. It is a hard taskmaster. Nonetheless, I now know that the pain, is somehow, essential to my health and wholeness.

What Do You Need?

The day Laurence died, my phone rang nonstop. The main question people would ask was, *"What do you need?"* I had no idea. I would respond: *"Please check with me in a few months. Laurence used to tell me that was the hardest time. I don't know what I need today."*

I am grateful for the few people who did check on me a few months later. Honestly, it did seem like most people disappeared. I guess they forgot or didn't realize what I was asking for at the time.

The one thing I did know that I needed early on, was a place for my feelings and my stories about us. But I didn't want to over-burden my friends with all my lamenting, so instead, I started writing. There were some nights when I did reach out to friends, sobbing. But mostly I wrote these stories, one by one, as I remembered them.

Tolerating life's sorrows is a big challenge of being human. Paradoxically, it's also what brings us more fully into joy. We have to go *through* pain to get to the other side. We can't go around it. Another thing I had learned in that graduate class in 1989.

Losing Laurence gave me an opportunity to be with grief again with whole new eyes. Congruent. Real. But mostly really hard!

A few months after Laurence died, I sent out a professional newsletter, listing suggestions for helping someone through grief (see appendix iii.) I wrote it because I had no idea what I needed when Laurence died, and I thought making a list might help others in the future with the task.

Recently I was talking with a man who just lost his brother to cancer. He told me that the one thing he hates the most is when people ask him what he needs. In the early stages of grief, or even later, it is very hard to know. Please DO NOT ask: *"What do you need?"* Instead, show up, shut up, and listen, with NO judgement *or* advice. And always *BRING SOUP!*

Some of my friends offered herbal supplements and other remedies to help me feel better. The message I derived from those offerings? *My grief was bad.* Much like when my father died. Today, I know my feelings aren't bad, but rather they're essential, if I'm to be fully alive.

I didn't need remedies. I simply needed people who were brave enough to be with me and my emotional pain.

Elizabeth Kubler-Ross, a pioneer in grief, compiled a list of five stages of grief. These include denial, bargaining, anger, depression, and acceptance. They don't necessarily occur in linear time but come and go throughout the grief process. Knowing this helps me to understand the feelings as they arise.

During the first few weeks and even months after Laurence died, I was in and out of denial and bargaining. It all seemed so hard to take in. I blamed myself for being apart from him. The biopsy confirmed that he had died of an enlarged heart. I read about *broken heart syndrome*, which can result in an actual physical heart attack. I was worried that leaving him alone after having lost his wife three years prior had been too much for his heart to take. I was bargaining. If only I could have loved him enough to keep him alive.

The anger I felt when we were apart the few months prior to his death was part of my grief as well. I was angry when he died, but the big anger had already happened during the separation/preparation.

Depression is the hardest part.

I can't help but wonder if the ninety-day separation was actually a preparation for his death. We loved each other so much, and at times had no idea why we needed such harsh measures to deal with our codependency. But, we somehow just *knew*.

When I imagine what it might have been like if he had died when we were in the early stages of *bliss*, I see myself barely able to survive. The time apart gave me a chance to begin my grief while he was still here, so the shock wasn't quite as profound.

Nonetheless, it was still acutely overwhelming.

And, at the time I had NO idea what I needed.

My Magical Mystery Ride

Shortly after Laurence died, a friend shared with me a hunch she had about the theme song from *Love Story* that had been playing in her head all week. She couldn't seem to get the tune out of her mind, and then she heard it playing on the radio. She couldn't help but wonder if it was a message from Laurence.

Curiosity got the best of me. I immediately ordered the movie on-demand. When I noticed the film was released in 1970, the same year that my father died, I remembered why I had been uncomfortable watching with it my mom that year.

As I watched the movie again, I thought about the love that Laurence and I shared. It seemed completely fitting that he would want me to watch this movie and see the story of two people sharing a few years together deeply in love. We were such romantics. I loved loving him. He loved loving me.

I couldn't help but wonder if my mom had something to do with me being prompted to watch this movie. Then, I pondered many things.

How do people communicate with their loved ones after they die? Are Laurence and my mom orchestrating some grand design for me? Is this just some crazy joke? What was happening?

The synchronicities that have happened since Laurence's death, and even before, have reopened many questions for me about this life and beyond. When my father died, I was angry because everyone was telling me he was in Heaven, and I should be happy. I wanted to go to Heaven. I wanted to be able to be with him. Why does God get to have him and not me?

I spent my whole life seeking Heaven and God, trying to find my father. Even though I was raised Catholic, I couldn't accept that a Man in Heaven had taken him to a better place.

My lifelong spiritual search led me to books and classes about God and Heaven. I attended lectures, took classes, went to see psychics and mediums, and met with spiritual teachers and guides. The summary of what I've learned is that God is the *love that never dies.*

In 1988 I read a book by Jane Roberts titled, *The Nature of Personal Reality.* Channeling an entity named Seth, she shares insights into how we create our own reality. It was the first book that seemed to answer my questions about life and death. The book explains that what we believe in will appear when we die. For example, if we believe Jesus will greet us in Heaven, then that's what we'll experience. Kind of like a dream.

I will never forget my mother's face the morning she died in 2008. Her big, blue eyes were wide open in wonder, and she had a huge smile on her face. I imagined she saw angels and the Blessed Mother taking her to my father. What a delight to see her smiling as if she had found her home.

I recently watched a PBS special with physician and author, Deepak Chopra, titled, *You Are the Universe.* Chopra ponders questions of matter and consciousness. He states that only ninety-nine percent of the Universe is visible. The rest is invisible. When I think of it that way, I realize there's so much more out there than what we can see with the human eye.

A few years ago, a colleague of mine was studying between-life regressions, based on the work of Michael Newton. She asked me if I would be interested in doing a session with her as part of her training. She guided me through a meditation where I was completely relaxed and prompted to be aware of my surroundings, in a *so-called* in-between-life state. I saw an infinite supply of golden light swirling around. It seemed to be the essence of All That Is, always available for us to use for personal growth, fulfillment, and vitality.

It felt congruent with what I had been assimilating, related to Heaven and God. I had come to the conclusion years ago that God was an infinite and always available energy of love and light. Not a He or a She, but just pure love. How, then, does that energy communicate with us?

I guess some things just have to be left as a mystery. I refer to my life as a *magical mystery ride,* because one of my significant discoveries in my spiritual search was the recognition that being fully alive requires living in *the unknown*. If we knew everything, then we wouldn't have the day-to-day experiences of wonder and exploration. It is paradoxical however, in that living in the mystery means we have to have trust we will be okay, even without knowing how. Hard for us humans who like to be in control and in charge of everything!

Laurence knew how to live the mystery. He held a deep faith and shared a spiritual understanding similar to mine. That was certainly a large part of our attraction to each other. We prayed and meditated together. We shared our dreams together, and we both trusted and valued our intuition.

After he died, a good friend reminded me that the spiritual connection we had while he was alive will certainly continue, even though his physical body is gone.

That feels true.

The Bedroom Slippers

I dreamed of my father almost every night after he died. For a very long time. It felt like we were together again. Then, I would wake up and realize that it had only been a dream. Every morning, a stark reality. My father was gone. At first the dreams were comforting. Over time, they became unsettling. A continuous reminder of what I had lost and would never regain.

I kept the dreams a secret because I wasn't sure what people would think or say. Talking about my father was a taboo subject. I feared what might happen if I did. I stayed silent.

I felt that my father was truly visiting me at night. The dreams were so real. They began with the sound of his leather slippers sliding across the floor. It was a familiar rhythm, similar to a slow and steady dance. One, two; one, two... as if a doorbell was ringing to say, *Hello I'm here, please let me in!*

I loved his nighttime visits. After all, it was all I had left, or so it seemed.

The Sunday afternoon after Laurence and I watched the Broncos game, *the week before our official first date,* I stopped at Costco on the way home. In the very front of the store was a display of cozy slip-on slippers. I had been in need of bedroom slippers for quite some time, and even though I was on a limited budget for the ingredients needed to make my traditional pumpkin cake rolls for Christmas gifts, I bought myself the slippers. I've worn them every day since.

Recently, when I was getting into the bath, I looked at the slippers on the floor. The dreams I used to have about my dad flashed before me. Then, I remembered the day I bought the slippers. I thought about the stories Laurence and I had shared, and the excitement and hope of us possibly beginning something new and wonderful together.

I noticed how very worn out the slippers had become over the past few years. It seemed a subtle reminder of my father, and my time with Laurence; both worn-out, yet still very comforting. I suppose one day

I'll need to replace these slippers, but for now I still do the slow dance slide across the floor each morning. The love and comfort of those memories will never go away, nor can they be replaced.

I wondered if buying those slippers that day was an accident, or if it was all part of this crazy dream of life and death that keeps showing up as synchronicity. I suppose it's, again, another mystery.

Impermanence

Weekends were especially hard after Laurence died. Jigsaw puzzles became my refuge from the intensity of the early shock. After completing my third seven-hundred and fifty-piece jigsaw puzzle, I broke it up and put it back into the box.

It was a reminder to me of the impermanence of being. I thought of Tibetan sand mandalas. After a week in meditation, chanting, and ritual, while creating intricate geometric designs with colored sand, the monks destroy the mandala. They bless the sand, sweep it up, and disperse it into a nearby body of water as a blessing. Many people feel uncomfortable as the artwork is being destroyed. It tugs at the heartstrings of those who want to hold onto everything, as if that's a choice.

Mandalas are a type of meditation practice. After my divorce in 1996, I signed up for a class taught by California mandala artist, Paul Heussentaum. He taught a drawing technique using black paper, colored pencils, and stencils. The process of drawing mandalas helped me get out of my head and into my heart. My nervous system relaxed into this ancient art form.

I value the mandala drawing process so much that I now teach mandala classes and use mandala drawing in my personal and professional life.

But back to the puzzle.

As I took each of the puzzles apart and placed the pieces back into the boxes, I was reminded that nothing lasts forever. The puzzles again broken into tiny little pieces.

Grief.

Nothing lasts forever.

April Fool's Day

April Fool's Day, 2017. I guess the joke is on me. I had no idea that this was the way things were going to go. Sometimes, it does feel like a bad prank or a bad dream that will end when I awaken. You know the feeling when you wake up from a nightmare, relieved it was only a dream? That is how I feel. Maybe one day I'll wake up and Laurence will be here in my arms again because it was just another bad dream. *April Fool's.*

Likened to the dreams I had after my father died, Laurence sometimes comes to visit, too. Sometimes it is comforting; sometimes it is deeply saddening. I wake up and realize it was just a dream. Laurence is dead. Stark reality again. Here is one of the dreams:

Laurence and I are together again after our ninety-day separation. We are happy to be together and very clear about us. No more doubts or ambivalence. I know that the ninety days has been a good thing for him and me, and we have more gratitude than ever before about being together. We hold hands as we always did. We walk and talk and play together just like before, only now even more solid and clear. We walk over to a tree-like podium that has a sign-up sheet for a Mile Hi event. When we get to the sign-in sheet, there are no more pages left. A woman tells us to put our initials at the end of the last page to hold the spot until she can get more pages.

The feelings in the dream were nice; as if everything we had been trying to achieve in our relationship had happened. We had arrived at a very strong and solid place of being together in a healthy and mature way. We both knew the separation had helped, and that we would never take each other for granted, ever again.

The relationship cancer was cured.

Waking up and realizing I would never get that opportunity was one of the hardest moments after he died. No longer will we hold hands; no more competitive Scrabble competitions; no more nights in his arms. The silence was maddening.

The morning after the dream, I sat in my living room, as I always do, to write down my dreams, meditate, and pray. Typically, the quiet moments bring me comfort. That morning the silence hurt. The aloneness chilled me to the core. I wanted Laurence to be sitting beside me so terribly. The pain was brutally intense. Here is a poem I wrote about the silence:

This Silence
This silence is too much.
"Enough," I say.
Stop this madness.
Bring on the celebration.
Let this lamenting end.
Bring me my lover.
Breathe life into me again.
Break open my wounded heart.
Let me love again.
For I must, or I too will die.

Shadowlands

I recently re-watched the movie *Shadowlands* starring Anthony Hopkins and Debra Winger. It's based on a love story about the famous writer, C.S. Lewis, who lost his mother when he was nine years old. A well-known female writer, played by Debra Winger, develops a close friendship with him. After much time witnessing his resistance to more than a friendship, she calls him out on his avoidance of a relationship saying: "You have created a world where no one can touch you."

After losing my father, I, too, had created a world where no one could touch me.

Shadowlands is a great title for a movie depicting the loss of a parent, which can easily result in a fear of abandonment and/or a closed heart. Carl Jung, a well-known psychiatrist, named the parts of ourselves that remain hidden in the unconscious due to our fears, *the shadow.*

C.S. Lewis, played by Anthony Hopkins in the movie, said, "We live in the shadowlands. The sun is always shining somewhere else" (Attenborough, 1993).

Jung's explanation of how the *shadow* can impact us makes perfect sense in light of unresolved grief. If we are unwilling to face the discomfort of grief, it will stay in the *shadow* and affect us in other ways, such as unexplained anger, depression, fear, addiction, etc.

At the end of the movie, Lewis reflects on his life: "Why love if losing hurts so much? I have no answers anymore. Only the life I have lived. Twice in that life I've been given the choice. Once as a boy I chose safety, and once as a man I chose suffering" (Attenborough, 1993).

I believe that the romantic love I shared with Laurence helped me grow up, so to speak. I'd been stuck as a twelve-year-old little girl, afraid of losing and being abandoned again.

Nonetheless, my idea that Laurence was a *safe bet* was simply an illusion.

I have to grieve the loss of my father, and now Laurence, *on my own.* In this process, I come face-to-face with my *shadow.* This is a continued life-long journey of individuation and wholeness. Even though fairytales portray *happily-ever-after* with another person, the truth is: the stories represent our inner wholeness, *not* a search for *the other.*

In his book, *We: Understanding the Psychology of Romantic Love*, Jungian psychologist Robert Johnson (2009) wrote about romantic love:

> When we are in love, we believe we have found the ultimate meaning of life revealed in another human being. We feel we are finally completed, that we have found the missing parts of ourselves. Life suddenly seems to have a wholeness, a superhuman intensity that lifts us high above the ordinary plane of existence." (p. xii)

However, Johnson (2009) further explains that romantic love is never as much about the other person as it is about each individual's growth and evolution:

> Romantic love is the mask behind which a powerful array of new possibilities hides, waiting to be integrated into consciousness. But what has begun as a huge collective surge of psychic energy must be perfected at the individual level. It is always the role of the individuals to complete the task, to bring the divine process to fruition within the microcosm of our own souls." (p.4)

Laurence gave me an opportunity to step into my fears in a way I had not done before. But the truth is he couldn't have been the one to heal the deep wound I developed after losing my father. I had to be able to face my inevitable fear of loss, in order to step more fully into loving myself, or anyone else, for that matter.

Losing both my father and Laurence to sudden death was extremely traumatic.

However, the big lesson I learned was: *true love is letting go.*

That's the deal.

It's Common to Idealize the Dead

It's seems easier to recall the good times with Laurence more often than the bad. The way he used to fix me breakfast, call me *darling*, take care of me when I was sick, listen to me talk for hours, open the car door, treat me with respect, and all the other wonderful things that man offered to me daily. He truly was a blessing.

However, several people pointed out that I might be idealizing the relationship. They reminded me of the struggles we had in our second year, and the challenges we would have if he were still alive.

In the same graduate class that I mentioned earlier, I would write weekly *thought papers*, that reflected events in my life. In one of the papers, I wrote about my father. The instructor's feedback was "It is common to idealize the dead. You might want to balance the scales a bit on the memories of your father."

As I recalled this feedback, I wondered what would have happened if Laurence and I had gone on our next date? Would we be working on our differences related to urban versus country living? Would we find better ways to communicate and work through conflict?

I'll never know.

Another dream I had after Laurence died was about a woman I've never met in waking life. She told me that even though Laurence had made a commitment to himself to remain outside any relationship for ninety days, she had a feeling he was attracted to her and she thought he might ask her out after the ninety days. I said out loud in the dream, *"It's a good thing Laurence is dead, because if he was alive, I would have to kill him."* The dream reminded me that we had much work still to do on our relationship, and it had been far from perfect.

Nonetheless, he was a remarkable man. I was telling a friend recently that Laurence gave me some non-negotiables for my next relationship. I won't allow a man to treat me with disrespect ever again. I want my man to go the extra mile to make me happy. My man will put our relationship first. I will *not* settle for less.

Laurence Freedom is a hard act to follow.
Still, he was not perfect.
No one is.

You Should Be Ashamed of Yourself

A few months after Laurence died, I went to Denver and had dinner with our friend, Jim. Talking with Jim about Laurence brought loneliness to the forefront. Driving home on that rainy night without Laurence, for yet another weekend, was hard.

Somehow, it felt shameful to still be in this place of sadness.

I was the youngest in my strict Catholic family, and always a bit naïve and innocent about things. When I continually heard, "You should be ashamed of yourself," I began to think there was something wrong with me for being curious and innocent. So, I attempted to stop being *me.*

When my father died, and no one wanted to talk about his death, I wasn't going to bring it up and risk hearing the words, "You should be ashamed of yourself!" Instead, I held my sadness in silence. I didn't want to tell anyone because it seemed as if my brother and sister were doing fine.

I was truly *ashamed of myself.*

Losing Laurence gave me pause to reflect on how I might grieve differently now that I am an adult.

Reaching out one night on Facebook, I mentioned how I worried about burdening my friends with my grief. One reassuring response was: "A burden is assumed, not placed. Grieving is a process which occurs over the course of a lifetime, it is a part of you and you will learn to hone its sharp edges."

Another one, from my sweet friend DeAnn: "You can burden me anytime. I love you and with that comes my unending support." And from Karen: "I am here for you—not a burden—and you will be there for someone else when the timing is perfect—take all the time you need."

Those posts reaffirmed that grief my is okay. I don't have *anything* to be ashamed of. I'm *not* a burden. And, I'm not a *mistake.* I know that now.

Get Over It

When I saw Brené Brown speak the week before Laurence died, one of the things she shared in her lecture was that we should put a ban on limiting how long a person can grieve. She said that grief takes as long as it takes, and in order to completely grieve, forgiveness has to happen. Laurence and I were in a place of complete forgiveness the last night we were together. I am so grateful for that.

As I grieve, I notice my guilt and my fear of being self-indulgent for feeling sad. Again, back to my early years when I was told to be happy because my father was with God. The incongruences and ironies of that time remain in my somatic body memory.

In my training and work as a therapist, I've learned that it is best to breathe deeply into that memory and remind myself it's okay to feel whatever I'm feeling. If I need to cry, I cry. If I need to be alone, I'm alone. If I need a friend, I call a friend. I pay attention.

This is actually how we grieve a loss to completion. We have to go through it. We can't go around it, or it will stay stuck in the somatic memory.

So instead of staying stuck, I wrote these words.

I have no idea what this grief will look like going forward. One day at a time. When people ask me how I'm doing, I can't find words to describe how my grief and my life are simultaneously doing a strange sort of jazz-rhythm dance. I know I won't be in deep grief forever. I know that everyday something seems a little better. Still everyday there is another reminder of what I will never have again. Another sadness to be felt.

That's the way grief goes. I won't rush it. I'm letting it take the time it needs. It has much to teach me, if I remain open and listen. I'll get over it when I'm over it. Not a minute sooner. And I know that is okay.

IKEA and the Shaman

A few months after Laurence died, I scheduled a healing session with Gary, the shaman who used to work with Pedro. When I found out that Gary was continuing to offer healing sessions without Pedro, I signed up with him right away. It seemed significant in light of the fact that Gary had lost his business partner, and I had lost Laurence, both to heart attacks.

Gary lives in Taos, New Mexico. He and Pedro came to Denver several times a year to perform shamanic healings for people from our church. Now Gary continues the work on his own without Pedro.

When I met Gary that Sunday, we shared our stories of grief, and then he did some healing work on my broken heart.

I planned to go to IKEA after the session was over since I don't often get that far south of Denver. I enjoy the unique and affordable options offered there, and I needed containers to organize my kitchen cabinets.

Laurence hated IKEA, mostly because of the way the store is designed. Once you start along a path, it can be challenging to go backwards due to the traffic flow and the store layout. I think he felt a bit trapped in there.

Part of the healing with Gary included a visualization of Laurence and me exchanging flowers with each other as a way to say goodbye. I smiled as Laurence led us in a dance. We circled around in a way that when he was alive, would often have made me dizzy. However, this time I wasn't dizzy at all. I was able to spiral around in the energy of the love that we shared, and I knew that we would always be together.

After the dance, we exchanged our roses in such a way that our arms formed a figure eight. It made me think about Mary Magdalen since the number eight is often associated with her. It's also the infinity number, which to me, means our love will never die.

I said goodbye to Laurence, and then my thoughts wandered to my upcoming trip to IKEA! I felt a bit ashamed for thinking about IKEA during this sacred healing time.

Gary then told me that Laurence and I have a soulmate connection that will never die, and he emphasized the deep love that we share. He said that we've probably had many lives together and will most likely meet again. Then he made a comment about how important it is for me to let him go, and for me to move forward. I laughed, as I wondered if IKEA may have *actually* been relevant.

Was Laurence's sense of humor reminding me that once you start down an aisle, you have to keep going forward? Was he reminding me that we can never go back?

Just like IKEA?

The Wedding Vase

On one of our dates, Laurence and I went to a Native American Pow-Wow in Denver. He wanted to buy me a gift. He loved to buy me presents. I often felt uncomfortable receiving so much from him, as I wasn't used to allowing men to spoil me the way he did.

I suggested that we buy something for *us*, instead of *me.* He agreed. As we looked around at quilts, dream-catchers, and other possible items we could share as a couple, I spotted a hand-made wedding vase made of clay. Laurence hadn't asked me to marry him yet, but the vase still felt right for us. He bought the vase, and we happily brought it home to sit upon the mantel.

I sometimes imagined how we might actually use the vase one day in our wedding ceremony. In Native American tradition, one spout of the vessel represents the husband and the other represents the wife. The looped handle represents the unity of marriage, and the space created within the loop represents the circle of life. In the wedding ceremony, the groom offers the bride the vessel and she sips from one side. The bride then turns the vase clockwise, and the groom sips from the same side. Then they each drink from the opposite side, and then both drink from it together. If the couple can do this, they will have a strong marriage.

Since Laurence and I never got to our wedding ceremony, the vase was not put to use the way I had imagined it might be. After he died, I wondered what to do with it. I knew it would always be a reminder of our *marriage* of sorts, but I also knew that it might not be appropriate for me to hold onto it, as my life has to move on eventually.

I thought of John and Vanessa.

They were married on April 8, 2017, the day before what would have been Laurence's sixty-third birthday. I wasn't able to make the trip to Brazil to attend the wedding, but I wanted to get them a gift. As I was thinking about what I might choose to send them, the wedding vase came to mind. I felt a bit conflicted as I really didn't want to give it away; but on the other hand, it seemed so perfect for them. I wanted John and Vanessa to have this precious vase that represented how much Laurence loved me, as a way to acknowledge how precious their marriage is, and how much they both meant to Laurence.

I mailed the package to Brazil. I had never mailed anything out of the country before. I had to fill out customs paperwork and declare a value on the item. The postal worker told me it would take three to four weeks to get there and the postage was quite expensive. I was a bit concerned that it might never make it to John and Vanessa, which would bring great sadness to me. Yet, somehow, I knew it was the right thing to do, and I also sensed that Laurence would keep an eye on it to be sure it arrived.

That was another huge piece of letting go. Even though I knew it was the right thing to do, I experienced more grief as I said goodbye to that memory, and the item that represented our *marriage*.

Vanessa sent me this message after the vase arrived:

"Thanks a lot for the beautiful vase! You won't believe me, but when we were in Colorado we almost bought one to bring home, but we did not because we could not put more weight in our suitcases! Guess u guessed it! Thanks a lot; it means a lot to us and I can see why Laurence would like to give it to us, too! So beautiful and with such a special meaning. Thanks and lots of love. John & Van"

Hope

On the five-month anniversary of Laurence's death, I was in Palo Alto, California presenting on the topic *Positive Psychology*, for PESI, a continuing education organization.

The Friday before, I had been asked to fill in for an instructor who had a personal emergency.

I agreed to take on this arduous task in return for an extra day in Northern California to see my two youngest children and my five-year old grandson. PESI agreed to the extra travel day, and I was off Saturday morning to California.

I had breakfast on Sunday with my children at a place called Renata's Creperie. It's my favorite place to go when I visit my daughter. Renata is an artist, and the walls are filled with her artwork. Since I'm gluten-free and dairy-free, the menu is terrific. An almond chai and a bacon, avocado and egg gluten-free crepe made for a very nice Sunday morning. It also happened to be Laurence's birthday. He would have been sixty-three years old that day, April 9, 2017.

I'm sure he wouldn't want to be any older then he was when he died at age sixty-two. He really didn't want to age. I always reminded him when he was eligible for senior citizen discounts. He hated that.

Laurence had been to Renata's with us two years prior when we had taken the trip for my daughter's graduation and birthday; the trip when we stopped at Confusion Hill.

My children and I toasted Laurence at breakfast, remembered him fondly, and smiled. It seemed odd and sweet all at the same time; one of those moments when it's hard to find words.

After breakfast I got on the road to Sacramento where I was going to present the first day of *Positive Psychology*. About halfway there, I passed Confusion Hill. I wanted to stop, but I had to get to the hotel before dark and prepare for my talk. I knew that the memory of the time spent there with Laurence would always be with me, and I didn't need to revisit the place in order to keep it in my heart. It was time to keep moving. Bittersweet.

One part of the *Positive Psychology* presentation related to hope. As I was talking about *hope* with the class, I recalled another mysterious incident that happened after Laurence died. When Laurence moved out of our Niwot home, he left a few boxes of his Christmas decorations in my garage. Most of the ornaments were from his marriage to Suzan, and no one had much interest in them after he died. I took a few pieces out that specifically belonged to us, and then took the rest to Goodwill.

A few days later, I opened the trunk of my car and saw a shiny, silver star that had fallen out of one of the boxes. When I picked it up, I saw it had the word *HOPE* on it.

I don't think that was an accident.

I believe Laurence was telling me to have *HOPE*.

Another very profound and vivid dream also happened on that trip. The night before the training, I dreamed that Laurence was curled up behind me. In the dream, I reached back and touched him in the hope that he would stay with me longer. I had a feeling that he was really with me, even though I knew he had died. I wanted to ask him questions about what it's like after we die, but I didn't want to waste the little bit of time we might have together with questions. When I turned around to look at him, he smiled and said, *"I am really here."*

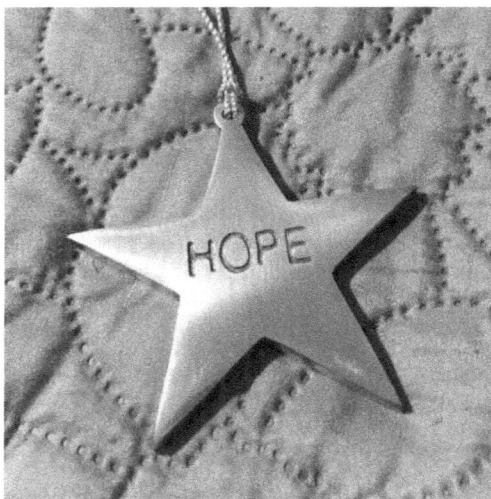

Romance Angels

Laurence and I had a magical relationship. It allowed me to feel loved in a way I'd never felt before. It pushed my edge related to receiving love from a partner. Laurence was solid and good to me. He taught me much about how to give and receive love.

The week before Valentine's Day, my friend who had the hunch from Laurence about the movie *Love Story*, told me she sensed Laurence telling her that he was putting *romance angels* around me.

He wants me to move on, she said.

That Sunday I tuned into Doreen Virtue's weekly angel card-reading on YouTube and was surprised to find her working with the *Romance Angel* cards that day. I had no idea that romance angels were a real thing.

I ordered the *Romance Angel* card deck and a *Romance Angel* CD from her website. As much as I believed that grieving takes as long as it takes, and as angry as I was at Laurence for wanting me to move on, especially since he never really got over his wife while he was with me, I decided to be open to possibilities.

I remember when Laurence and I were dating, several of my women friends said, "It's so wonderful you found love at your age." I was always a bit shocked at that comment because I had never really thought about dating and relationships as having an expiration date.

Then, I started to notice that many women my age are single, either by choice, or lack of any good prospects. I felt even more grateful for Laurence. After a lifetime of healing from losing my father, finally my man had arrived.

Several of my friends who are deeply intuitive have mentioned they see me in another relationship. Even Gary, the shaman said it, adding, "When you're ready, of course." I find some comfort in hearing that because I'd like an opportunity to continue what I was opening up to in my relationship with Laurence. Since I certainly can't continue with him, the only other option is living this life on my own, and/or trusting that I can love again.

I imagine that Laurence is helping me do just that by sending me romance angels!

He always wanted me to be happy.

Of course, he would want to help me find my next true love.

From Fear to Love and Love to Grace

After Laurence's wife died, he began working on a program he called *From Fear to Love, and Love to Grace.* Carolyn Myss, in her book *Invisible Acts of Power*, says that *grace* is *gratis*—meaning a gift. Furthermore, she defines theological grace as "...unmerited divine assistance, aid given to help us regenerate our spirits and lives—a virtue coming from God" (p. 16).

In my spiritual seeking, I discovered that grief gives us an opportunity to open up to something greater than ourselves. It deepens us. How we respond is our choice. Grace comes after we move past fear into deeper love. Only then can we experience *grace.*

I suppose *grace* is really what I was referring to that night in Laurence's new office when I shared the quote with him: *Break my heart open to a higher love.*

Having been raised Catholic, and later in my life studying the archetype of the divine feminine, I learned about *The Immaculate Heart.*

Images of *The Immaculate Heart* often portray a wounded heart with light shining brightly outward from the edges. To me, that means that even though our heart is broken, there is always a greater light that continues to shine. When we are willing to fully embrace the pain, we discover the eternal part of us that can never die.

Saint John of the Cross, a fourteenth century mystic talked about this in his book *The Dark Night of the Soul.* St. John speaks about how his inward journey into spiritual darkness was ultimately what allowed him to experience divine love and new light.

Laurence's heart was deeply broken as he endured three major losses in a short period of time. His experience of moving from fear to love and love to grace was his daily practice.

He started each day with "The Prayer of St. Francis" (2018):

> Lord, make me an instrument of Your peace;
> Where there is hatred, let me sow love;
> Where there is injury, pardon;

Where there is doubt, faith;
Where there is despair, hope;
Where there is darkness, light;
And where there is sadness, joy.
O Divine Master,
Grant that I may not so much seek
To be consoled as to console;
To be understood, as to understand;
To be loved, as to love;
For it is in giving that we receive,
It is in pardoning that we are pardoned,
And it is in dying that we are born to Eternal Life.
Amen.

Next, he would make a pot of coffee and run a bath. He connected to Spirit in the water. After his bath, he would write in his journal. It's from there that his writing of love and grace began.

From his inspired writing, he began offering classes in his new office and giving talks at conferences on love and grace in addiction treatment.

I edited some of his writing, so I'm grateful to have his words on my computer. I know he would want me to share them.

Here is the beautiful introduction to his class:

I want to welcome you to this JOURNEY of LOVE. The Meditation/Heart Space model you will be learning came to me one day in my own meditation practice. Since receiving it, I have practiced the principles of focusing upon love and holding a loving heart 'HEART SPACE' to test out my belief that being, having, holding, and extending a loving heart will bring GRACE into my life. This practice has been almost a year in the making with incredible results. I am now ready to pass this meditative model on to others and share the gifts it brings when practiced.

In the workbook, he continues on to write more about love:

Essence of LOVE is an expression of the Infinite Source. LOVE is eternal, always was, always will be, and always available at any time we choose to open to it. *By joining with LOVE, we come into contact with our true essence of being made in the image and likeness of the everlasting. Simply stated, there is nowhere that God/LOVE is not. I am love, you are love, and we are loved. We can feel and believe that we are separate or cut off from God/LOVE, but this is never the case. Like the small water drop in the ocean we are surrounded by God/LOVE, we are in it, it is in us, we are small particles of God/LOVE floating in and making up the vast endless sea of infinite God/LOVE. Returning to LOVE is returning back to the Source of all life and returning to our true nature— LOVE.*

Laurence recognized how getting out of his thoughts, or what he called the *head space* allowed him to move through fear to love, to deeper love, to the heart space, and then to grace. He created this graphic for his workbook to illustrate this idea:

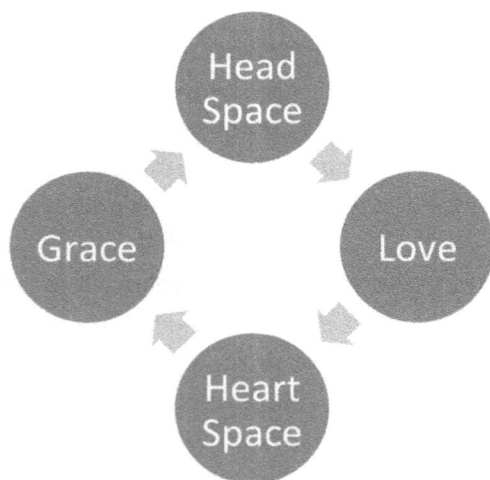

And, here is a little more of what he wrote about the power of love:

Love is the universal language we can relate to, no matter the background, nationality or language spoken. Love motivates us to take risks and go past fears to become great. Love will lift up and empower others to transform. It is LOVE that is remembered when a lifetime passes. It is LOVE that causes us to sacrifice our own welfare for another and it is LOVE that reflects our greater selves. LOVE is powerful because LOVE is the essence of all life in the Universe. LOVE is God in action.

When we align with LOVE, we are using the Infinite Creative Power and Intelligence of the Universe to create a life of greater possibility. Simply stated: All things are possible, if we believe that the Infinite Universal Power of LOVE is real and is working with and for us to fulfill our deepest heart's desires.

The most powerful time in a life is NOW; the past is a memory, the future a distant wish. Fully showing up in this moment, bringing your heart into this moment, speaking, feeling, responding to your life in this moment, is where all of life resides.

Aligning with LOVE, moment by moment is aligning with the creative Power of the Universe. It is in the moment that inspirational thought fully realized and believed moves possibility from an idea to a physical reality. When a moment is energized with the Power of the heart all things are possible.

A Legacy of Love

Elisa, the medium who Laurence went to see after he lost Suzan, called me a few weeks after he died to share two important messages she was getting from him.

The first one was about our ninety-day separation. When Laurence and I first started dating, he told me he was going to live to be ninety. He seemed healthy and enjoyed life. We both were confident he would be around another twenty-eight years.

Laurence wanted Elisa to let me know that *living to be ninety,* instead referred to him living until the end of our ninety-day separation. At first that felt comforting, and then after more reflection, it felt like Laurence's way of saying that he was right. He did have a competitive edge about him. I had to laugh. He would have thought it funny, too.

The ninety days had been a preparation. He died pretty close to the mark. He knew somewhere deep inside he was going to hurt me. His soul knew he was leaving, but neither one of us could have actually known he was about to die. Again, the *mystery.*

The other message that Elisa had for me from Laurence was that he was listening to *our song* when he passed. Elisa asked me if he had ear-buds in when he died. He did. I'm guessing the song she was referring to was "Make You Feel My Love." The one we danced to in his apartment when we were first dating, and later frequently referred to as *our song.*

Additionally, the week after Laurence died, I contacted my friend Wendy in Virginia. Wendy works similarly to a psychic or medium; however, soul-blending is what she labels her readings. She's a very wise and authentic woman. I'm so grateful to have met her twenty-plus years ago shortly after my divorce. She helped me understand unconditional love and other aspects of the soul self.

I haven't talked with Wendy much since my move to Colorado twenty years ago. She knows very little about Laurence and our relationship. After he died, I called to see if she could give me a message from him. Here are the notes I took during the phone call:

A long-term relationship was not in the cards for us. I was planning on leaving, and it helped for us to separate. I did not want to change plans and I really wanted to spend time with you. It was unique. I left because of me, not you. I didn't want to hurt you. I felt deeply happy and free. I was recreating, resetting and revamping myself with you. I had a lot of emotional problems and couldn't get over Suzan due to my childhood trauma and my emotional immaturity. I could not move on, even though we had a soul connection. It was juxtaposing two things. I wanted to marry you authentically, and I never satisfied that.

I was hoping separation would shake things up.

Many souls transitioning now are passing over to a huge transmigration, evolving as a species. The solar system is expanding as a race. Spiritual beings are being called.

I had a sense of something BIG, but my soul didn't want me to have the details. I love you and trust you and I am trying to connect with you. The rational mind wants to make sense of grief. It's just change. Nothing is the way it used to be. It's important for you to ask the following questions:

How does the soul make me aware?

How do I react?

How am I different?

You are free to experience this. Love self. Be different. Be yourself. I will applaud you. Take this as a wealth of expansion, a treasure trove. This experience will give you insights. You will remember me as a companion you knew well. It is not a loss. I have given you material to help others.

The light has changed.

Increase your self-love, and have compassion for yourself, not grief.

At the end of the call, I told Wendy that I was going to speak at Laurence's memorial service in a few days. I asked her if there was anything Laurence wanted me to say on that day. She responded, "Make them chuckle, help them connect, and let them know I'm leaving a legacy of love."

I hope I met those requirements in the eulogy, and I also hope that my writing this book fulfills them even further. He truly has left us all a legacy of love that never dies.

As I conclude this writing, I am reminded of what Laurence wrote after he almost died in Mexico. Possibly it was the lesson he needed to learn in order to let go and move on to wherever he is now:

What I have learned is that I am not alone and that I have an army of invisible helpers from the other side standing by me that love me. By surrendering I am guided, I am cared for, I am protected, and I am carried into a greater life of possibilities that far exceed my deepest dreams and desires.

Maybe that is **grace.**

APPENDIX

Appendix i

Laurence Freedom Memorial Service Eulogy
November 22, 2016

Two years ago today on November 22, 2014 Laurence and I had our first official date. One year ago today on November 22, 2015, Laurence asked me to be his wife. When Dr. Patti called me last week to tell me that the *only* day the church had available for Laurence's service was November 22, I immediately thought *Laurence must have had something to do with that!* What I make up in my mind, is it's his way of reminding me how special I am!

I met Laurence nineteen years ago, when I first moved to Colorado. He was an expert at networking with people. I remember the first moment I shook his hand and heard his name, Laurence Freedom—I thought, *what a powerful name.*

"It's so nice to meet you."

Our paths continued to cross at work when we shared an office space at Colorado Counseling Professionals and also when we ran into each other here at Mile Hi Church, which we both call our spiritual home.

When Laurence opened the Freedom Center, he had arrived at a pinnacle in his career that fit him well and stroked his passion for helping people in recovery. He was so good at that. I was always in awe of how he could convince people to get into treatment. Having been in the counseling field for over twenty years myself, I know it's not an easy task. People trusted and respected Laurence. He saw the light in everyone and people felt his kindness and genuine compassion.

I always admired Laurence's commitment and devotion to his beloved wife, Suzan. I saw him as a man of deep integrity and truth. When Suzan died, I remember sitting in this sanctuary, crying deep tears for Laurence. I had not known Suzan well, but I knew how deeply he had loved her.

Laurence and I went on our first official date one year after Suzan died. We moved fast into a serious relationship. One thing about Laurence is he always moved fast. That is evident even today as we all sit in awe of how quickly he passed! The way he liked to do everything. Fast.

Laurence took me to Hawaii less than two months into our relationship. We planned the trip three weeks after our first date and I remember saying at the time, "I'll be glad when we hit the one-month mark, so I can at least tell people we've been dating for a month instead of just a few weeks when I say you're taking me to Hawaii." Not that either one of us cared much about what anyone else was thinking. We both knew it was right, and it was so very right. It was a magical trip. One evening we literally stood face to face, hand in hand, between the sun setting on one side and the moon rising on the other. Laurence loved that night. He would often say it was the universe lining up to affirm how right it was for us to be together.

Early in our relationship we had our astrological charts read and learned that his Aries sun and Cancer moon was the direct opposite of my Cancer sun and Aries moon. This made us extremely compatible, as well as extremely oppositional at times. It was quite a combination. The loving aspects of Cancer allowed us to both shine in the realm of home, family and love. We loved to be in love and we both loved family and being together. I had never met a man who was as generous and kind and caring. He would have done anything for me. And he was happy to do it. Our Aries nature, on the other hand, at times gave us some problems. We were both very strong-willed, stubborn, and competitive. We had an ongoing Scrabble competition where he kept a record of our final scores on his phone. He was so proud to always be able to say his high score was 384, and that the closest I ever came to that was 341.

We didn't argue much, but when we did, it was always about our opposing beliefs about how to argue!

Nonetheless, Laurence was my best friend. I knew I could count on him for anything. We shared everything together and had a kind of love that was sacred and profound.

Laurence touched the lives of hundreds and hundreds of people, as you can see from the number of people here today. He radiated un-conditional love and pure light. He loved with a depth of heart that is precious and rare.

Every morning he began his day with the prayer of St. Francis. Every evening he ended his day with a prayer of gratitude.

I have no idea what the next chapter of my life will be like without him. I do know that he left a legacy of love that will live on forever in my heart and all of yours The day he died, I felt as if I heard him say, "I can take even better care of you from here. You are going to be okay. I am always with you." I know that's also true for all of you out there who are feeling, and will continue to feel, that missing piece of your life known as Laurence Freedom.

I want to close with a message from Laurence that he wrote for his workbook:

You were an expression of love before you were born,
you will return into love when you pass.
Between your first and last breath,
your true mission is to remember the love that you are
and to extend this love to all those around you.
LAURENCE FREEDOM

Appendix ii

Denver Post Obituary
LAURENCE FREEDOM
1954-2016

Laurence Freedom M.Ed., CACIII, LPC, LAC, MAC (birth name-Larry Ratcliffe). Born in Denver, CO, to Bill and Mary Ratcliffe. Laurence passed peacefully in his home. He worked in addiction treatment, founding and operating the Freedom Center in Lakewood, CO. He touched and helped many recovering from addiction and trauma. He is survived by his son Colin Ratcliffe, siblings Nora and Ed Ratcliffe. Laurence is preceded in death by Suzan Freedom. Memorial service will be held at Mile Hi Church in Lakewood on Tuesday, Nov. 22, 2016, at 10 AM. Donations can be sent to Mile Hi Church, 9077 W. Alameda Ave., Lakewood, CO 80226.

Published in the *Denver Post* on Nov. 19, 2016

Appendix iii

Suggestions for Helping Others with Grief

"What do I need?"

The first few days after my partner died people asked me, "What do you need?" I had no idea at the time. I thought about that question months later and created this list for anyone wanting to help someone during grief.

- I don't know what I need the first few days, weeks, or even months, so don't ask.
- Please keep calling after the first week has passed.
- Don't ask me to get over it and move on.
- Let me be sad.
- Let me be weak.
- Let me be vulnerable.
- Call me at night when I am alone and say hello.
- Send me flowers.
- Cook me meals.
- Offer to help with bills that don't get paid due to bereavement time off.
- Let me cry.
- Give me lots of hugs.
- Massages are always welcome.
- Let me tell you the stories of us, over and over again.
- Be patient.
- Don't give up on me
- Please don't ask me to be strong.
- Let me take as long as it takes.

Appendix iv

A Child Needs Extra Help with Grief

Death is extremely difficult for everyone to accept. Adults sometimes want to shelter children from pain by not talking about death. This is the worst alternative because telling the story will actually help a child work through the stages of grief.

Some things to remember when talking to children about death are:

• **Avoid euphemisms**, and always tell the truth. Children need to know that the person is never coming back. Expressions such as "sleeping," "passed on" and "left us" are confusing and should be avoided. Instead, use honest terms such as "died," "he stopped living," "his body stopped working," "he had a very bad disease." Use phrases that do not misrepresent the reality of death and that the child can understand.

• **Encourage the expressions of emotions**. Many feelings are going to come and go during the grief process. Anger is part of grief, and children may need outlets to express it. Let them be angry and sad. Don't try to make them feel better but give them the freedom and space to feel what they need to feel. Remember, it takes time to move through the stages of grief.

• **Explain what is going to happen**. Children can participate in the ceremonies of saying goodbye to someone who has died. A family member or close relative should explain the different places and events as gently as possibly. Talking through the services and the burial rituals will help the child understand and say goodbye in a way that works for him or her.

· **Make a "memory album."** As time passes after a death, the child may want to make a memory album. In the book he/she can draw pictures, write letters, and place special memorabilia. This memory book helps to keep that special someone alive in the heart.

· **Use caution when discussing religious beliefs.** Telling a child that God or Angels have taken a loved one can be frightening. The child may fear that will happen to him/her. Even though religious beliefs can be comforting at the time of death, the words need to be chosen carefully. Avoid images that will create additional fear, fantasies, or anger.

Children who are grieving need strong support from those who can help them get through the pain and make them feel safe and secure. Death isn't easy for anyone, but if you can help a child remember the special person in his life, you are sharing the gift of memory. That is what remains after the pain.

Appendix v

Grief Resources

Judy's House, Denver, Colorado
www.judishouse.org
Former NFL quarterback Brian Griese lost his mother to cancer when he was a teen. Brian struggled with his grief for many years. He and his wife, Dr. Brook Griese, a psychologist specializing in childhood loss, started Judi's House in 2002. The program is designed to provide a safe, comfortable place for children and their families to come for compassionate support and connection.

Death as a Spiritual Teacher with Dr. Patty Luchenbach
www.milehichurch.org/CoursesWorkshops/DeathAsASpiritualTeacher
A transformational workshop that provides the opportunity to use the awareness of death as a teacher in our lives. Explore grief, loss, and growth of the soul experienced in our many encounters with death, both psychological and physical. We honor death as part of the process of transformation. Contact Patty to do a workshop for your group or help you with individual healing. http://pattyluckenbach.com

Canyon Hospice, Boulder, CO
www.theboulderhospice.com
An organization of professionals familiar with the challenging decisions involved in end-of-life care, who can walk with patients and families at these times.

Appendix vi

Relationship Resources

The Hoffman Institute
www.hoffmaninstitute.org

A week-long residential and personal growth retreat center in California that helps participants identify negative behaviors, moods, and ways of thinking that were conditioned in childhood. The Process helps you become conscious of negative patterns of thought and behaviors in order to make significant positive changes in your life.

Imago Relationships
www.imagorelationships.org

This transformational method of therapy was developed in the 1980s by Dr. Harville Hendrix and Dr. Helen LaKelly Hunt, and provides resources for couples, therapists, or individuals seeking to find a way to be more effective in their life and relationships.

The Meadows Treatment Center
www.themeadows.com

Located in Tuscon Arizona, the Meadows Treatment Center helps individuals with the emotional and relational trauma related to codependency better understand unhealthy coping patterns.

The Bridge to Recovery
www.thebridgetorecovery.com

Located in Kentucky, the Bridge to Recovery is designed to unlock trauma and underlying issues related to codependency.

References

Andrews, L. (1993). *Animal Speak: The spiritual and magical powers of creatures great and small.* St. Paul, MN: Llewllyn Pub.

Ashley, P. (2014). *Living in the shadow of the too-good mother archetype.* Deadwood, OR: Wyatt-MacKenzie Pub.

Attenborough, R. (Producer), & Attenborough, R. (Director). (1993). *Shadowlands* [Motion picture]. United Kingdom: Spelling Films International.

Barellis, S. (2013). *I choose you* Lyrics © Sony/ATV Music Publishing LLC.

Bradshaw, J. (1988). *Healing the shame that binds you.* Deerfield Beach, FL: Health Communications.

Bradshaw, J. (1992). *Homecoming: Reclaiming and healing your inner child.* NY: Bantam Books.

Bolen, J.S. (1995). *Crossing to Avalon: A woman's midlife pilgrimage.* San Francisco, CA: Harper-Collins.

Chopra, D. (2017). *You Are the Universe: Discover your cosmic self.* NY: Harmony.

Dylan, B. (1997). *Make you feel my love* Lyrics © AUDIAM, INC.

Folsom, R. (2013). *Back of my heart.* Boulder, CO: Sunshine Productions.

Hays, J., & Watts, M. (2017). Remember Mary Jane bread? The Norfolk bakery no longer exists, but the scent is sealed in local memory. *The Virginian-Pilot.* Retrieved from https://pilotonline.com

Johnson, R. (2009). *We: Understanding the psychology of romantic love.* NY: Harper One.

Kubler-Ross, E. (1969). *On death & dying: What the dying have to teach doctors, nurses, clergy & their own families.* NY: Scribner.

Mayes, F. (1996). *Under the Tuscan Sun.* NY: Broadway books.

Myss, C. (2004). *Invisible acts of power: Channeling grace in everyday life.* NY: Atria paperback.

Negri, P. (ed.).(2003). St. John of the cross: *Dark night of the soul.* Dover Publications

Nielsen, K. *The Princess and the Pea Exposed.* http://artpassions.net/stories/princess_and_the_pea_exposed.html

Roberts, J. (1994). *The nature of personal reality.* Novato, CA: New World Library.

Sibley, B. (2015). *Through the Shadowlands: The love story of C. S. Lewis and Joy Davidman*. Ada, MI: Revel Pub.

Sternberg, T., & Wells, A. (Producers). Wells, A. (Director). (2003). *Under the Tuscan sun*. United States: Touchstone Pictures.

The prayer of St. Francis. (2018). *Our Catholic Prayers*. Retrieved from https://www.ourcatholicprayers.com/the-prayer-of-st-francis.html

Vaughan, F. (1995). *Shadows of the Sacred*. Wheaton, IL: The Theosophical Publishing House.

Virtue, D. (1999). *Healing with the angels oracle cards*. NY: Hay House.

Virtue, D. (2012). *The romance angels oracle cards*. NY: Hay House.

Wheeler, C. (2016, March 16). If I die before you. In William R. Pringle, *Cheryl Wheeler*. Retrieved from https://cherylwheeler.com/songs/ifidie.html

Williamson, M. (1999). *Enchanted love: The mystical power of intimate relationships*. NY: Touchtone.

Acknowledgements

Where can I begin to say thank you?

I am so blessed to have family and friends who continue to love and support me every day. From the moment Laurence died, Junia called me every day to check on me and began filing in the void of Laurence's voice calling me *darling*. Every call started with *"Hi, darling."*

DeAnn was there on Thanksgiving night, when I wailed and couldn't stop the tears.

And, everyone else....

Thank you from the bottom of my heart.

Joan Schaublin was one of my editors, as well as my late-night friend. She shared with me her experiences of grief, and she supported me all along the way. Writing a book this vulnerable takes courage. She told me it was good, and I should DO IT!!

My sweet friend, Donna Remmert read the book many times, through several revisions; continuing to cry, while telling me it was good. I thought she was just being sweet Donna, but after Joan's encouragement, I decided to do this thing. This vulnerable narrative of love, loss, and grace.

To all the people who allowed me to use their names and share these stories. Most of the names in the book are real, with the exception of a few who asked to remain anonymous.

Thank you Nancy Cleary for believing in me again and publishing this very intimate memoir.

And thank you to everyone else out there who opened their heart and risked being vulnerable with me. I love you all!

About the Author

Dr. Patti Ashley is a mother, educator, author, and psychotherapist. With thirty-plus years in these roles, she has developed a well-seasoned approach called *Authenticity Architecture,* where she helps individuals, couples, and families break-through barriers to personal freedom and authentic growth.

Her self-proclaimed *magical mystery ride* of grief began at age eleven, when her father died of a sudden heart-attack. She continued this journey as her marriage ended, her children left home, and her amazing mid-life man-of-her-dreams died of a heart-attack, two years after their first date.

Patti is skilled and inspiring, demonstrating that even with tremendous loss *thriving* is the goal, not just surviving. She offers in-person and on-line counseling and educational seminars on mothering, grief and authentic relationships. She also leads individual and group experiential retreats in the United States and Europe.

www.pattiashley.com

www.ingramcontent.com/pod-product-compliance
Lightning Source LLC
Chambersburg PA
CBHW020158090426
42734CB00008B/860